FROM SLEEPLESS IN SEATTLE TO I SEOUL YOU

Seuta'afili Patrick Thomsen PhD

FROM SLEEPLESS IN SEATTLE TO I SEOUL YOU

Korean gay men and cross-cultural encounters in transnational times

The Queer and LGBT+ Studies Collection

Collection editor
Seuta'afili Dr Patrick Thomsen

LPp

First published in 2023 by Lived Places Publishing
Copyright © 2023 Lived Places Publishing
British Library Cataloguing in Publication Data
A CIP record for this book is available from the British Library
ISBN: 9781915271242 (pbk)
ISBN: 9781915271266 (ePDF)
ISBN: 9781915271259 (ePUB)
The right of Patrick Thomsen to be identified as the Author of this work has been asserted by them in accordance with the Copyright, Design and Patents Act 1988.
Cover design by Fiachra McCarthy
Book design by Rachel Trolove of Twin Trail Design
Typeset by Newgen Publishing UK
Lived Places Publishing
Long Island
New York 11789
www.livedplacespublishing.com

ABSTRACT

Queer worlds are often theorized using Western frameworks of knowledge systems and power. In this book, queer author and researcher Seuta'afili Patrick Thomsen brings diversity to the discourse by exploring the stories of Korean gay men in and between Seoul and Seattle. Drawn from lived experience and the author's use of *talanoa* (Pacific research methodology), the book centers transnational, migrant, and racialized realities – so contributing to the complication of West-centric ideas of gayness and coming out.

Looking at the intersections of race, globalization, diaspora, religion, and queer identity, these stories add richness and complexity to the field of queer and LGBT+ studies.

KEYWORDS

Queer; Seoul Korea; Seattle; diaspora; migration; gay; coming-out; talanoa; race; racism; racialization; transnationalism; globalization; decolonialization

This book is dedicated to all the Korean gay men and queer Koreans I encountered on this incredible journey. Without you, I am nothing as a researcher; without your stories, and your generosity in sharing them with me, this book and my academic career would not be possible. Your bravery and courage continue to inspire me every day. And to all my friends and family in Korea, your love sustained me throughout my entire decade living in your wondrous and heavy country. May all your dreams come true. And to my mum, for being my champion even in times of darkness.

This book was kindly reviewed by Dr Daniella Shaw, Birkbeck University.

Contents

Chapter 1 Beginnings   1

Chapter 2 Sleepless in Seattle: The complex
and complicated coming-out process   33

    Discussion questions   52

Chapter 3 Doing the transnational time
warp: Constructing difference between Korean America
and contemporary South Korea   55

    Discussion questions   71

Chapter 4 Global Korean gaze: Influences from
the "West" and the emergence of a Korean gay
consciousness in Seoul   73

    Discussion questions   96

Chapter 5 Negotiating queer/gay futurity in Seoul   99

    Discussion questions   113

Chapter 6 Seattle so gay white: Unpacking
the experiences of racism among Korean gay men   115

    Discussion questions   130

Chapter 7 Insidious collusion: Exploring
the transnational nature of gay racism   133

    Discussion questions   155

Chapter 8 Conclusion: Thoughts and reflections from a
Samoan queer researcher   **157**

References   **173**

Recommended further reading   **185**

Index   **187**

1
Beginnings

Every story has a beginning, and the research I share with you in the following pages begins on a fateful late Seoul summer night in 2013. At the time, I was happily living in a two-bedroom villa in the Itaewon[1] district, set within the heart of the foreigner district. I was a 27-year-old Samoan kid from South Auckland who had found themselves in the Korean[2] megacity through a series of fortunate coincidences. That night, I was waiting for my boyfriend outside Dangsan subway station with a sense of dread and anxiety coursing through my veins. In recent days, after a weekend away at his family's home outside Seoul, his messages had turned suddenly cryptic.

Before he left, we were in high spirits, joking around with our usual ease and sharing passionate and hidden kisses. As a gay couple in Seoul, and an interracial one at that, we knew it best not to be visible in a society we both understood would struggle to understand us. I hadn't seen him since he had returned, and I could sense something was wrong. His messages became labored with effort and evasive in their lack of frequency. Phone calls went unanswered and were subsequently unreturned. Although it had only been a couple of weeks since we had seen each other, it was clear to me that something was seriously wrong.

When he arrived that night, with head and eyes lowered under the cap he always wore out of his work clothes, I knew my instincts hadn't failed me. Without so much as a hello, slowly, he opened his mouth and said the words I knew were coming: "I think we should break up."

I went numb and felt the air grow heavy around me. My center, or what we call in Samoan my *moa*, became unsteady and queasy. My fight mode activated, and my lack of experience in dealing with very public break ups shone through as I struggled to make sense of what was happening. I could feel a mixture of rage and grief welling in my throat.

"Why?" I shouted back furiously. "We haven't even had a single argument, and you know I love you, and you always say that you love me. This doesn't make sense to me. Are you not happy with me? What have I done?" During my emotional outburst, he continued to remain silent and somber, standing directly in my firing line without flinching. When my extensive verbal barrage finally subsided, he said, in a quiet and strained voice: "I think we should break up."

Exasperated at this point, I pressed again, not understanding the heaviness he was carrying with him as his eyes began to gently water.

Bewildered by what was happening in front of me, I made such a scene that the endless streams of people floating about us seemed to take notice, and I could sense their secondhand embarrassment for me as they scurried away, trying not to make eye contact. Many were hurriedly getting on and off trains mere meters from where we stood and could easily hear what was going on. I didn't care.

I felt like my world was falling apart right in front of me and I was prepared to fight for it, or for my dignity at the very least. "If you want us to break up, you better give me a good reason. If you've found someone else, just say that, so I can move on and know that you were a complete waste of time."

Those words seemed to break the spell, and he responded firmly this time, but I couldn't be sure of his exact words. My entire being froze as I was forced into stunned silence. "It's not anything you've done," he said. "We need to break up because I have to find someone to marry. This society will never accept us, not now, not in the future, and I'm the eldest son, it's my duty to my family."

I truly felt like I was in some sort of K-drama at this point. Wounded beyond recovery, my head began to spin, and I knew I had been defeated.

Most PhD journeys don't begin as tumultuously and dramatically as mine did. And although the hand of fate would intervene many more times before I finished my doctorate in 2018, I can honestly say that the work I share in the pages of this book can trace its beginnings to that painful and fateful night under a bridge in the western part of Seoul's subway network. I was a graduate student then, studying toward my Master's in International Studies degree at Seoul National University. I had been in Korea for about five years and had some sense of the difficulties faced by gay men in Seoul, as I, too, had encountered the pressures of a heterosexist Korean mainstream on the decisions I had made around my own sexuality and the levels of visibility I chose to share.

At that stage of my life, I felt like I lived in two completely unrelated Korean worlds. I was a well-respected teacher and high-achieving graduate student by day, and a raging homosexual frequenting the bars of Itaewon's homo hill by night. There was an uneasy balance I felt in living a life moving seamlessly (and dangerously) between different publics. And I began to realize that in this precariously exciting liminality I had come to enjoy, I had neglected to develop my own understanding of what it could possibly mean to be gay for Korean men in Korea. As an outsider, I could never *really* know an experience that I did not embody, but I realize now that, at times, I had somehow forgotten that I also carried the privilege of having acceptance within my own family and culture; a privilege that wasn't afforded to the men I met, loved, and ultimately fell into relationships with.

Following my cringeworthy public break up debut, and once the dust had settled a bit, I became intensely interested in understanding more deeply the world I was living in as a gay Samoan; as a spectator-participant, beginning to seek out explanations to unanswered questions that emerged after that night. The journey from that heated evening outside Dangsan station to this doctoral work took many twists and turns before I left Auckland via San Francisco to begin the story of this research in the twilight of the 2015 Seattle summer.

Drawing on my own lived experiences of living in South Korea for seven years before I arrived in Seattle, and as a transnational Samoan engaging in and trying to make sense of a complex form of my own transnational mobility, this work began with a simple question. I wanted to know: what were the factors that impacted Korean gay men's decisions around sexual visibility? How did these factors come together and were any factors more pertinent than others? Put another way, what was it that made it difficult for many of the men I had encountered to come out? Further, did this calculation change when they moved countries, considering the increasingly global nature of queer mobilities? In many ways, it was my attempt to work out how I could get to a closer understanding of the men whom I encountered during my time in Korea and the US, who struggled with coming out and claiming a gay identity or subjectivity in a public space.

Many explanations I found in the literature I studied gestured to things one would expect to find. Often, cultural pressures, including the omnipresent power of Confucian social, political, and familial norms, had constructed a heterosexist society and heterosexist state formations that marginalized any expressions of queerness or gender and sexual non-normativity in Korea (Chase, 2012; Cho, 2009, 2011). Christianity also appeared to exert a strong influence over the way that all these factors moved with and against each other. Unique among the big three (China, Korea, Japan) in the northeast corner of the Asian continent, South Korea bore the hallmarks of a long entanglement with Christian missionaries that had been seen by many as a modernizing force (Clark, 1986; König, 2000).

Reducing the complexity of the processes of marginalization to cultural factors and Korea's specific version of Confucianism, I found, is an unsurprisingly simplistic explanation. As Dongjin Seo (2001) notes in their essay *Mapping the Vicissitudes of Homosexual Identities in South Korea*, homosexuality in Korea had been eternally deferred; a term without a reverent and subjected to Orientalization from within. Exploration of homosexuality in Korea had been caught up in the suffocating pace of change affecting Korean society. Homosexuality is intertwined with the complex historical context of Korean sexuality, which itself has not been the subject of widespread conscious exploration and reflection. In other words, sexuality in Korea as a whole has been under-studied in reference to the wider social shifts that accompanied Korea's rapid move toward industrialization during the Park Chunghee dictatorship and the push for greater globalization in the 1990s.

Seungsook Moon (2005) would offer one of the most significant critiques in this vein following Dongjin Seo's important work. Moon's conceptualization and coining of the term "militarized modernity" made significant strides in bringing a gender critique to the history of Korea's rapid industrialization, also known as the Miracle on the Han. Moon argued that in producing and reproducing a heteronormative state formation under the Park Chunghee dictatorship, the Korean state weaponized and deployed a lens of crisis economics to construct Korean women as docile reproduction tools, while Korean men became militant citizens designed to protect the interests and integrity of the South Korean state against North Korea and outside forces. Therefore, any questions and explorations around gender, and by extension sexuality, were also repressed under a discourse of protecting the nation. This troublesome heteronormative form of statecraft and state building is what Todd Henry (2020) would refer to as survivalist epistemologies, where questions around gender and sexual diversity are constantly deferred to ensure the survival of the South Korean state amid a discursively formed shroud of foreign imperial and neocolonial forces. This shrewd discursive practice continues to govern and restrict calls for greater integration and protection for South Korea's gender-

and sexual-diverse populations. The militant strand embedded within the arm of the Korean state apparatus is draped heavily over the way Korean gay and queer communities can live out their lives in contemporary Seoul.

In this book, I use the term Korean familism and variations of it as a tool to mark out theories that exist around the shape and function of the Korean family institution. Many foreigners are familiar with Confucianism, and in the Korean context, the Confucian family tradition. This tradition centers on patrilineal succession, preserving rigid relationships between father and son; historically, it has proven to be most successful in maintaining strict social order. For example, the Family Register Law was established in 1960 to prescribe regulations on one's legal domicile and the head of the family and family members. Under this law, a patriarch as head of the family was recorded first, and following this were lineal ascendants of the head of the family, a spouse of the head of family, and then lineal descendants of the head of family and their spouses (Yang, 2013). Derived from a Confucian tradition that was established in the second half of the Joseon Dynasty (1392–1910), this strict adherence to Confucian norms is often assigned as a key barrier to the integration of gay men and queer communities in South Korea (Bong, 2008; Seo, 2001).

Notably, though, Chang Kyung Sup (2011) advances the idea that as Korea experienced intense social and political turmoil over the past 200 years, major shifts also occurred in the Korean family. Through Japanese annexation, colonial subjugation, and the disastrous Korean War, Korea suffered from a dissolution of traditional order, leading to a disintegration of stable state governance. As such, Koreans developed familial relationships and structures of reliance to fill the vacuum of security that a stable state apparatus could not provide through social welfare. This again would shift under new pressures placed on the Korean family unit following rapid industrialization, the military dictatorship and a new drive toward global competitiveness and cosmopolitanism.

Chang Kyung Sup tracks these changes through a pluralistic understanding of the Korean family that bears hallmarks of what he terms **instrumental familism**, **affectionate familism,** and **individual familism**. Instrumental familism describes how, due to perpetual state instability and the building of structures of Confucian familism, Korean families mobilized resources and kin networks for social, material, and political advancement out of necessity. In reference to affectionate familism, Chang adds that following Korea's large-scale industrialization, this form of familism emerged as a result of highly educated women remaining home after marriage and becoming more exposed to Western forms of family-making practices. Affectionate familism engenders stronger care bonds between parents and their children that can transgress the rigidity of prescribed roles that Confucian familism encourages. In this book and on this research journey, I found that bonds between participants and their parents became a central site of knowledge-making and understanding in relation to questions I sought answers to.

Following on from this, with a generation rising in South Korea from the mid-1990s with no recollection of the hardships of the military dictatorship or Korean War, there came a developing thirst for cosmopolitan credentials to increase individual competitiveness within Korea's globalizing society, underpinned by neoliberal urgencies framed within meritocracy. There are now multiple generations, post-dictatorship era, that have been assaulted by glitzy advertising and an e-information highway via the Internet, raised and completely immersed in an ultra-competitive, consumerist society. Kim terms this "the emergence of individual familism," which can lead to friction between generations who often desire different things. This is related to what Abelmann and colleagues (2013) term **Chaggi Kwalli** or a desire to cultivate the individual self in order to make one's self more competitive in a globalizing Korea. In this sense, for my own research, the idea that Korean families are conservative and just too Confucian to accept a gay identity – and by extension Korean society – is a reductive notion facilitating a need to examine carefully the socio-historical context in which narratives shared here are constructed. And indeed, what I was to find in the stories of participants was a much more complex reading of the role their families played in their own lives and articulations of a gay or queer subjectivity that went beyond these reductive labels.

Another force with a complex and layered history on the Korean Peninsula, as alluded to earlier, is Christianity. The role of missionaries in Korean politics and social trajectory is significant to this work. Christianity was successful in infiltrating the religious practices and political trajectory of Korean society by aligning itself with political movements that positioned Christianity as a modernizing emancipatory force, decoupled from its colonial underpinnings. According to Clark (1986) and Baker (2016), unlike in other locations where Christianity became associated with colonizing forces, Christianity in Korea became associated with a new kind of nationalism during the time of the Japanese occupation. Not only that, but prior to the Korean Peninsula coming under Japanese control, Christianity was adopted as a revolutionary edict, providing educational institutes and creating key infrastructure like hospitals and schools for people that were traditionally excluded by the *Yangban* (aristocracy). It even found its most fertile ground in Pyongyang: an area whose people were seen as uncouth and backward by their countrymen further south in Seoul. However, considering the long history of Christianity on the Korean Peninsula, many (including participants I encountered) believe that Korea's Christian groups adhere to stricter norms and ideals around gender and sexuality, than Christians in other Asian countries which many participants felt impacted their rigidity on gay and queer rights. Further, Christian fundamentalist groups continue to harass queer rights activists, movements, and festivals throughout Korea to this day.

The social and political upheaval of Japanese annexation, the Korean War and period of rapid industrialization, and the pursuit of a militarized modernity and neoliberal globalization also had a profound impact on Korean migration to the US. According to Bong-Youn Choi (1979), there are three distinct waves of Korean migration to America post-1900 and prior to the *Seghyewa* (Global Korea) period. The first wave (1903–1949) began when ship-loads of Korean migrants comprising mostly laborers and picture brides arrived in Hawaii, with the majority having been converted to Christianity in the Incheon area by American missionaries. These migrants established the first Korean Methodist Church in Honolulu. Many more would move to California and cities on the West Coast, including Seattle. The second wave (1950–1964) came as a direct consequence of the Korean War, when thousands of Koreans fled to the US; following the lifting on the ban of Asian immigration in 1952, Koreans were able to become US citizens. In 1965, the third wave of Korean migration to the US began with the removal of the immigration quota system, when family reunification became possible. In 1976, roughly 30,000 Koreans moved to the US in one year. For many Koreans, since the mid-1990s, the move to the US has been motivated by educational and work opportunities, as is evidenced by participant narratives here. As will be seen in the rest of this book, this history of Korean migration to the US would have lasting consequences on how the men I encountered in Seattle framed, experienced, resisted, and even strategized how to navigate their sexual identities in relation to their Korean ones. Negotiating complex and multilayered familial relations tied not only to cultural context, but also to the complications of migration, religions, and experiences of racialization and racism, turned their stories distinctly transnational.

The divergent experiences documented here do not exist in geographic separation. Participant narratives also show how, despite migratory shifts in location, their engagement with ideas around sexuality and visibility bore a markedly transnational flavor. Korean culture and participants' understanding of it across the Pacific Ocean were both connected and disconnected due to temporal and geographic shifts and cultural crossings that were re-sutured in divergent and complicated ways. With Korea's aggressive push toward globalization in the 1990s, the era of the "hermit kingdom" on the south of the Korean Peninsula came to a vibrant and dynamic end. For Korean gay and queer communities, constructs and notions of progress on the rights of gender and sexual minorities entered into a productive relationship with queer and gay activist movements rooted in the Euro-American context, framed as the following of more global norms and a desire for progress. As such, I offer a racialized critique of queer mobilities tied to constructs of racialized modernity rooted in these queer worlds of the Global North. I argue that race and racism is now a palpable experience in Seoul that impacts how Korean gay men in this study were articulating desire and their expressions of queerness in important ways.

My understanding and use of the term race owes much to the incisive scholarship of critical race theorists Delgado and Stefancic (2017). Throughout this book, I regularly refer to categories such as race, racism, and racialization interchangeably, to complicate interpretations of what participants shared with me over the course of my fieldwork. However, these three terms carry important nuances. My understanding of race is of a socially constructed category that differentiates people in each society along essentialist markers such as skin color, language, nationhood, cultural affinity, cultural patterns, and productions, among many others; markers assigned by a dominant group to other another. As Delgado and Stefancic (2017) outline, race has no biological and genetic reality; thus, it is a category that is manipulated, invented, and discontinued when convenient. The process in which racial categories are constituted – an analytic I argue is capable of capturing multiple practices of othering along the lines of race – is what I refer to here as racialization. Racism, then, encapsulates process, symbols, discourses, and resulting societal structures and institutions, where the power to be able to racialize accumulates and is exercised by the dominant racial group over the racialized within a given society.

In this book, I also make an implicit argument about the racialization under examination here being tied to notions of American imperialism. We often understand racism and racialization through a local lens. However, proliferating threads and connections tied to increased queer mobilities, as well as globally circulating discourses around queer representation, allows racializing processes in one location in the world to travel to another. My position is that racism is (1) ordinary and not aberrational and (2) can travel globally through migration pipelines between nation-states, where power to discipline bodies and people's rests comfortably within nation-state apparatuses such as immigration policies, and through discourses of modernity that are yoked to proliferating norms around queer liberational politics. As such, shades of racialized modernity can be read through the narratives of participants in Seattle and Seoul that speak to both the interpersonal nature of racism and the structurally embedded and connected process of racialization that connects stories and experiences between two state apparatuses (South Korea and the US).

An important spinoff of critical race theory, which is also a key element in developing the theoretical lenses deployed in this book, comes in the form of the concept of intersectionality. Although the concept and term has made huge strides globally as an analytic, I gesture specifically to Black feminist scholar Kimberlee Crenshaw and her articulation and conceptualization of the term to help think through some of the complexities of the narratives shared here. Crenshaw's (1989) foundational article "Demarginalizing the Intersections of Race and Sex" spoke to the way Black women's lived experiences of discrimination and violence were often made invisible in the court of law. Specifically, Crenshaw did so by showing how legislation and judicial decisions in the US erased Black women's experiences by focusing on a construct of a woman as a White woman, and simultaneously focusing on the construct of the Black citizen as a Black man. Where these two experiences met, the law was incapable of seeing Black women, rendering Black women invisible. The idea of converging marginalizations working to make invisible people who inhabit these mutually constitutive social experiences gives much credence to the analysis that follows in these pages. In acknowledging the specificities of intersectionality as a framework to the Black woman's experience, my invocation of the term and concept is not intended as a label or identity framework; rather, by following the logics of converging marginalization that Black women scholars have carefully detailed, I argue that one can begin to see that at both at a structural and interpersonal level, Korean gay men in Seattle, and in Seoul, experience converging and intersecting marginalizations on different social axes that color their practices of sexuality and identity-making in unique ways.

Another theoretical thread that helps to tie this book together is the concept of homonationalism as articulated by Jasbir Puar. Puar's (2007) concept of homonationalism is particularly pertinent for readings of queer liberational discourses from a globality lens. Puar uses homonationalism to describe how the use of the term acceptance and tolerance for gay and lesbian subjects became a barometer for the legitimacy of, and capacity for, national sovereignty. In other words, Puar asks us to interrogate how the question of whether you treat your homosexuals well or not became a way to adjudicate the morality and right to govern of particular state formations. While the discourse of American exceptionalism has always served particular heteronormative nation-state formations, Puar's (2013) work focuses on how sexuality has become a crucial part of the articulation of proper US citizens across other registers like gender, class, and race, both nationally and transnationally. In this sense, homonationalism is an analytical category deployed to understand and historicize how and why a nation's status as "gay friendly" has become desirable in the first place (p. 336).

Puar's homonationalism draws on the concept of the new homonormativity developed by Lisa Duggan (2002), and the idea of assemblage theory she drew from Deleuze's work. In terms of homonormativity, Puar extends Duggan's focus on the imbrication of privatization of neoliberal economies and the growth of acceptance of queer communities (Puar, 2016, p. 321). Duggan explains how neoliberalism is also a type of sexual politics, albeit contradictory and contested, it is a type of politics whose defining feature is that it does not contest dominant heteronormative assumptions and institutions but upholds and sustains them while promising the possibility of a demobilized gay constituency and a privatized, depoliticized gay culture anchored in domesticity and consumption (p. 179). Puar builds on the concept of homonormativity to create the analytical concept **homonationalism**, which aims to critique how gay liberal rights discourses produce narratives of progress and modernity that continue to accord some populations access to cultural and legal forms of citizenship at the expense of the partial and full expulsion of other populations from those rights (Puar, 2016, p. 321).

Throughout the book, there are references also to the "West" and "Western" ways of knowing and being. I take well the point that the term "West" is often an empty signifier and catch-all for anything that exists outside of the cultural norms of Asia, and in this case, South Korea. However, it **is** a term that participants used voraciously throughout the research. For them, the West represented norms, ideas, cultural productions, media discourses, languages (predominantly English), people, and expressions of Whiteness that exist primarily in North America and Europe. Therefore, despite its slippery nature, and despite it being an unsustainable binary (West versus Rest) empirically, I believe it has much purchase as a reference for participants in this study to make sense of how to frame the power structures that surround their experiences and expressions of queer identities in relation to their Korean subjectivities (Thomsen, 2020).

Also, I use the terms queer, gay, homosexual(ity), LGBTQIA+, and other markers interchangeably. In doing so, I also acknowledge that there is much nuance that exists between all these terms and my understanding is not definitive nor prescriptive. In this book, gay refers to a social identity claimed by men whose sexuality favors the company of other men. Queer, on the other hand, speaks to a knowing disruption of the gender binary and all types of normativities associated with gender and sexuality that follows the heterosexual matrix. This book focuses on the experiences of gay men, though many gay men also exist within the capacious auspices of a queer social practice and refer to themselves as such. My use of both terms is a nod to the often blurry line between the two. In using the term thusly, I also acknowledge the very strong critiques that rightfully exist of gay men whose practices around sexuality and visibility seek to recreate a form of homonormativity that often sidelines the interests and expressions of queer women and trans communities. But despite these complications, all participants referred to either themselves as gay and queer in different moments or to the communities they belonged to as being queer or LGBT, LGBTQI+, or LGBTQIA+, allowing a movement and fluidity between the use of these terms **just** in this context. Homosexuality is defined and operationalized here as the physical practice of same-sex sexual relations. As gay men, the reference to a gay identity speaks to the social expressions of identity tied to sexuality; homosexuality, however, speaks only of same-sex sex acts, which is a distinction that can also sometimes become blurred. My use of various forms of the LGBTQIA+ acronym gestures also to the tenuous coalition of multiple identities that can sit under a queer umbrella. However, it is also representative of expressions of identity that challenge normativities of all kinds and is deployed here as such. Often, when acronyms are deployed in this work, it was a term that participants themselves or other researchers have used in their own work.

Notes on methodology: How can a Samoan come to know Korean gay worlds?

As a Samoan researcher and lecturer of global studies, questions around ontology (what is real?) and epistemology (how do we know what is real?) orbit in productive tension around my work. And in the context of this book, a legitimate question becomes: how can a Samoan come to know Korean gay worlds? In the social sciences at least, epistemological traditions of Europe and North America dominate the way we carry out the knowledge generation process. Yet, as a Samoan raised in New Zealand, how I came to know the world around me and my role within it is very much rooted in the cultural knowledges and epistemological traditions of my ancestors, in that ontology and epistemology cannot be meaningfully separated from each other (Fa'ave et al., 2022). I believe that for Pacific peoples and many Indigenous communities around the world, the idea that an objective social reality that exists beyond body and mind is not possible, as it is in the body where knowing is located, and reality is constructed in relation to all living things around us in a mutually constitutive relationality.

Therefore, uniquely, my project deployed a Pacific research methodological approach that sought to lean into my differences and experiences as a Samoan, and into moments of relational interaction with participants, as the genesis of knowledge generation. This project had no intention or desire to obtain an objective, definitive truth to define Korean gay worlds. Rather, I sought to operationalize my positionality and lived experiences as a way to open a slightly different window and as a lens to understanding, cross-culturally, practices of queerness within a context that shared many identity-making practices to mine. As a progressive Samoan, I possess strong critiques of colonialism and the way it continues to govern our people's relationships with other more powerful nations. As such, my intuition here is to seek a complicated, decolonial reading of sexuality that aims to decenter the role of researcher as the knower-of-all-things, and seeks to center participant words as a window into truth-meaning and knowledge-generating that challenges the hegemony of Western scholarship over sexuality research across the world.

Pacific worlds are mobile, collective, relational, multifaceted, and storied. There are many syntheses that can be gleaned between Samoan and Korean worlds in this sense. Specifically, in Samoan social customs, there exists what we call the *vā*, meaning the space where social interactions take place between people. Maualaivao Albert Wendt (1996) explains that the *vā* is the space in between; it is this between-ness, and not empty space; it is not space that separates, but space that relates, that holds separate entities together. Samoa's traditions and protocols explain the nature of a Samoan being as a relational being. There is myself and yourself, and through myself, you are given primacy in light of our collective identity (Tamasese et al., 2005). In other words, for Samoans, there is no me without you, for the self cannot be defined outside of family lineage, village ties, church connections, and genealogical ties. To foster these connections, a space of mutual respect must be created between all within society.

The relational aspects of the *vā* and its role in identity formation, then, I find congruent with a Korean worldview that also suggests that a Korean identity or articulation of the self is formed relationally rather than individually. In particular, the Korean language demonstrates this symmetry, where the lexico-grammatical structure is formally dependent upon social and interpersonal factors such as symmetrical/asymmetrical relationships, kinship, gender, age, profession/vocation/

trade, as well as socio-economic status (Kim and Strauss, 2018). As an example, Lee Hye-Kyung (2018), in the field of linguistics, states that in presenting oneself in conversation and social settings, Koreans select terminologies in their language that refer to the self and the other in accordance with the expected honorific norms of Korean society. Nearly two-thirds of pronouns for the self in Korean are self-denigrating (p. 64). Lee presents the example of a Korean king who referred to himself using the Korean word *Kwain*, which literally means "an insufficient person." In Samoan language, the deference accorded to others is considered an important part of respecting the *vā* and the interactions that take place relationally within it, tied to one's own social position and lineage. For my own research, this innate understanding of relationality provided me with a second sense in being able to understand the difference between a relationally formed identity and one that encourages the development of the self from an individualistic perspective.

To activate the principles of *vā* relations in the research process, I chose to deploy what I refer to here as *talanoa* dialogues: a method of inclusive, participatory, and transparent dialogue. A Pacific research methodology rooted in oratory tradition, *talanoa* overcomes methods that disempower participants, by legitimizing the exchanging of personal stories between participant and researcher that explicitly express feelings with them. Vaioleti (2006) defines *talanoa* as a conversation, a talk, an exchange of ideas or thinking, whether formal or informal. This flexibility allows people to engage in social conversation, which may lead to critical discussions or knowledge creation that allows rich contextual and inter-related information to surface as co-constructed. It requires researchers to partake deeply in the research experience rather than stand back and analyze. *Talanoa* requires the researcher and participant to know each other and develop trust and a sense of relationality that cannot be achieved through a formal interview setting.

Talanoa finds synthesis with phenomenological research approaches which focus on understanding the meaning that events hold for participants (Patton, 1991, quoted in Vaioleti, 2006). Although this may appear to be similar to narrative research, *talanoa* is different in that participants will challenge or legitimize shared information. Because *talanoa* is flexible, it provides opportunities to probe, challenge, clarify, and re-align. It should create and disseminate robust, valid, and up-to-the-minute knowledge because the shared outcome of what *talanoa* has integrated and synthesized will be contextual, and is not likely to have been written or subjected to academic sanitization (Vaioleti, 2016). In line with what Alan Bryman (2016) states in reference to qualitative research, in *talanoa*, the researcher is necessarily implicated in the data that is being generated.

Timote Vaioleti (2006), who laid out the blueprint for *talanoa* in Pacific education research, frames the methodology through the Tongan language, where *tala* means to talk, and *noa* refers to nothing or nothing in particular. Thus, *talanoa* is sometimes defined as talking about nothing and anything at the same time. In my experience, *talanoa* as a methodology has found much purchase within Pacific research communities in Aotearoa, New Zealand. This is because a pan-Pacific identity underpinned by shared cultural values across heterogenous Pacific peoples has formed due to the presence of multiple mobility pathways into the country from the Pacific Islands, facilitating a racially marginalized diaspora community and experience (Thomsen, Lopesi, and Lee, 2022). Thus, *talanoa* allows Pacific peoples and researchers to give value and voice to Pacific ways of seeing, knowing, being, and doing (Keil, 2021). Furthermore, not only have Pacific communities and knowledges been racially marginalized in New Zealand, but, by extension, this has also contributed to the erasure of the cultural embeddedness of Pacific queer worlds (Thomsen, 2022).

As a Samoan, and a queer Samoan at that, Vaioleti's (2006) Tongan framing of *talanoa* – although enormously useful as a transnational Samoan with New Zealand citizenship – does not fully align with how I experience *talanoa* as a site and tool for knowledge generation. I acknowledge that *talanoa* can mean to talk about nothing (and anything) in many contexts, but in my experience, this is not how many use *talanoa* in research, as there are major mediating variables that can shift the criticality of *talanoa*. For instance, as Moeata Keil (2021) indicates in her research reflections, this conceptualization of *talanoa* has not paid much attention to the gendered, relational space that governs Pacific societies. This is especially true of Samoa, where gender roles shape different levels of communication, formality, and comfortability, and dictate what can and cannot be said within the *vā tapū*, or sacred *vā*, that exists between men and women as an extension of the *feāgaiga*, or covenant between brother and sister.[3] David Fa'avae and colleagues' (2016) work also spoke of the practical dilemmas they encountered when attempting to apply *talanoa* as young researchers in contexts where participants were older, in a society (Tongan) where rank and position dictate one's expected social interactions and choice of speech. In referencing the concept of *vā*, which *talanoa* as a method is connected to in this context,

Lana Lopesi (2021) poses an important critique, questioning the embedded assumption of neutrality that underpins our articulations and practice of it. Lopesi implores us to ask what happens to those who are not partaking in *talanoa*; and further, to consider what becomes of those who are not even invited to be part of *talanoa* in the first place. Lopesi suggests that we need to carefully consider the sometimes romanticized notions of *talanoa* and *vā* in the research space as carrying decolonial urgencies targeted at imperial framings of our peoples, whilst not considering the internal power hierarchies that exist within our cultures that serve to marginalize many within.

As a Samoan, I have always experienced *talanoa* from a different vantage point; one in which we are compelled into *vā* for various intentional reasons. Often, families, villages, *matai* (chiefs), and even politicians hold *talanoa* to unravel the complexity of specific issues, relationships, and family crises that need to be brought back into balance within the *vā*. To be sure, it is not this type of *talanoa* that Vaioleti is emphasizing in the research space, and I am not challenging the validity of their important articulation of their work that has empowered an entire generation of Pacific researchers. However, I wish to offer my own unique conceptualization and operationalization of *talanoa* in this book. As a queer Samoan, I draw from two Samoan words that differ from Vaioleti's position. The first is *tatala*, which means to open, and the second is *nonoa*, meaning to tie things together. Thus, the type of *talanoa* I am speaking to is one in which complexity is unraveled through respectful, caring, and relational dialogue. It is complexity and a desire to heal, plan, or strategize that draws people into *vā*, compelling them to engage in *talanoa* to unpack and re-braid the plait of social cohesion to meaningfully include those that have been left out.

Melani Anae (2016) speaks of the need to *teu le vā*: to nurture and take care of the space in between researcher and participant; a relationship in which knowledge generated must be in service of those whom the research is being conducted with. In my context, *talanoa* is intentional in its purpose: it seeks to untie the knots of social relations that have become entangled through sullied relationships because of hurtful behavior. It also seeks to begin the process of re-braiding in those of us who have been intentionally left out. I purport that this approach is pertinent for the context in which this research was conducted, as both myself and the participants shared in marginalization due to our sexuality, whilst still being expected to exist in heterosexist worlds where our queerness is made to be invisible.

Drawing from this framing of *talanoa*, I understood my duty as a researcher to develop a genuine sense of relationality with participants and my duty of care to ensure their stories were respected and not overly surmised and analyzed; to trust the truth in their own framing of their experiences as the site of knowledge-making. I also shared my own story as a way for the participants to understand that my experiences, although unique to me, may be helpful in unpacking the complexity of their lives. Coupled with my own unique cultural context and background, my research approach sought to center complexity by letting their stories unfold on their own terms. This meant that I took the time to know my participants as people before attempting to interview or hold *talanoa* with them. In doing so, I approached our *talanoa* with a criticality that came from my own sense of knowing that queer worlds are marginalized, often violently, the world over. Partaking in *talanoa* was not only a way of sharing stories, but also a method aimed at untying some of the knots within which society has entangled our lived experiences. And in highlighting this approach, queering *talanoa*, to a certain extent, meant that I, as a transnational Samoan, was taking with me my own cultural context as a tool for diversifying the way we study and theorize sexuality in the queer/gay space.

In deploying this research approach, I also sought to bypass, as much as could be achieved within this context, the gaze of the Western researcher, and to avoid the trap of Orientalism and Occidentalism by connecting Samoa directly to Korea from the vantage points of an Indigenous-to-Samoa researcher raised in a settler colony (New Zealand). And although I acknowledge that my research approach does raise questions surrounding bringing a different cultural norm around knowledge generation into a space beyond the context it was developed, I am comfortable in the fact that Samoan and Pacific forms of knowledge generation occupy a marginal position in the scholarly community, often stripped of any power to challenge the hegemony of empiricist social science, whose modern incarnation finds its rise in enlightenment principles of Europe. To make the assertion that an Orientalist practice can be equated to the way I carried out this research is an erroneous one in my eyes. These reflections may be refracted through my lens as an outsider who spent a decade in Korea, but in following the principles of Pacific research methodologies and methods, I ensure the site of knowledge generation is connection and relationality, not pure observation and attempts at definitive objectivity. This work is only possible

because I am Samoan, and the type of knowledge generated through *talanoa* dialogue held with participants in Seattle and Seoul was unique to this relational, cross-cultural, and generative context.

In the end, I conducted and held *talanoa* with 30 Korean gay men, 20 of them in Seoul and 10 in Seattle. These men were predominantly in their early- to mid-20s, with the eldest participant in the study nearing 50, suggesting that quite a youthful perspective is captured in the pages of this book. Additionally, I only held *talanoa* with self-identified gay men of Korean heritage, thus, I concede that the findings discussed in this book have a clearly gendered element that does not pay enough attention to the experiences of Korean lesbian women and transgender Koreans. For this shortcoming, it would be incorrect to think of this book as representing experiences, both mine and participants, beyond this context. Furthermore, I believe that as a fa'afāfine and gay Samoan man, it is not my place to research in the trans and lesbian space, although I hope that insights provided here, albeit within a gay man context, can contribute to discussions around Korean queer worlds and offer others carrying a more appropriate positionality potential ideas for their own work.

Furthermore, as has been emphasized throughout this introduction, this research and this book are tied to a specific moment in time. This is a point that bears regular repetition as I do not wish this work to be lifted out of its context for other purposes of interpretation. But I do offer this as a makeshift time capsule of sorts, providing reflective incisions into a specific temporal aspect of the development of Korean gay and queer worlds. I conducted research in both Seattle and Seoul between 2016 and 2017 and would encourage readers to keep this moment in time at the forefront of their minds. This was pre-COVID-19 and the existential crises such as the escalating climate crisis and heightened geopolitical tensions in Europe and the Pacific that are currently afflicting the world today were only just beginning to emerge and grow in significance.

Many of these *talanoa* took place in and around Itaewon, where I lived for many years. As I came to wrap up this book, the immense tragedy of the crowd crush in Halloween 2022 had just taken place in an alleyway next to the Hamilton Hotel outside Itaewon Station Exit 1, where more than 150 young people, predominantly Korean but also many others from other nations of the world, lost their lives due to the tragic crowd crush. Itaewon Station Exit 1 is a pivotal meeting point of different experiences in Korea. Often, many participants in this study – my Korean gay friends and boyfriends over the years – would use Itaewon Station Exit 1 as a meeting place; one that also functioned as an entry point to a vibrant nexus of many worlds: gay, straight, queer; Muslim; transgender; American; military; Southeast Asian; South Asian; New Zealand; Pacific; and many more, coexisting in a space carved out of and in relation to American militarism and the long hangover of the Korean War. It was a place where those of us who did not fit in could find comfort in our queerness and expressions of difference. Although I am sure there will be many severe political ramifications for such a horrific disaster, I wish to acknowledge, remember, and honor Itaewon as a site of multiple histories and struggles for the Korean people. Specifically, I want to honor it as a physical site, with its seasonally humid summers and icy cold winter nights, where much of Korea's contemporary queer history is written; a place where we as foreigners and Koreans of difference all found love.

May all the victims of this tragedy rest in love and their families be comforted in the honoring of their memories.

Chapter outline

The journey of this book and research begins in Seattle, the Emerald City of the US Pacific Northwest. In the first chapter, I present insights into the ways in which participants navigate sexual identity, visibility, and coming out. Furthermore, the participants and I story the way issues of culture, religion, and the power of the Korean American Christian Church (KACC) engenders innovative practices of negotiation tied to the fortunes of participants' families. A story in which a relational responsibility to others leads to a strategizing over sexual identity, where participants and the family members they trust and are responsible to enact a narrative of convenience to negotiate the intricacies and conservative textures of the Korean American community in Seattle.

Related to this, Chapter 3 presents what I term here a transnational time warp, where participants who recently moved to Seattle engage with a form of Korean culture that they felt was stuck in a time capsule. Drawing on the histories of Korean migration to the US, participants challenge the singularity of a notion that proposes that a shift to the US can lead to a more open queer life as Korean gay men. Rather, they suggest that images and practices of the Korean culture they encountered were rooted in a snapshot of Korean social and political attitudes that belonged to a bygone era. Thus impacting their ability and desire to engage with the Korean American community and Koreans in Seattle, who presented to them as conservative and often homophobic and existing in a separate world to the queer America they saw in other spaces.

The next chapter of this book mirrors my movement away from the West Coast of the US and back to the pulsating heart of the Korean capital. In Seoul, I encountered participants who were savvy with the latest terminologies and symbols associated with queer life in metropolitan cities of the West. In addition to documenting how influences from outside the peninsula helped participants to formulate and constitute their own gay and queer identities, I argue here that these discourses offer a benchmark that queer activists can deploy as a way to condemn the violence of the South Korean state, by making use of homonationalist discourses and practices of the West to advocate for what Woori Han refers to as a type of developmental citizenship for Korea's sexual and gender diverse communities. As a result, participants inadvertently cast Korea as backward and in need of catching up to the West as a tool of agitation, adding complexity to how we view the impact of American empire and Western hegemony in global politics.

In the next chapter, I home in on the idea of negotiated futurities, with a nod to the narratives of convenience identified in Chapter 2. Drawing on the concept of *Chaggi Kwalli*, or cultivation of self-reliance, participants story the Korean family as a site of negotiation and possibility, suggesting that the Korean family has evolved to incorporate instrumental, affectionate, and individual forms, and is more dynamic today than what discourses of conservatism popular in prior literature in both the US and Korea can allow us to theorize. In this chapter, the issue of a militant Christian bloc's power to hold back progress for Korean gay men and queer rights is also explored. Participants' narratives point to the removal of this power as being key to allowing new possibilities to emerge for a queer futurity in their minds and lives.

As a Samoan researcher, in some ways my racialized presence impacted and shifted the direction of many *talanoa*, where I noticed a strong race inflection beginning to permeate participant stories. In Chapter 6, I offer a snapshot into how participants in both Seattle and Seoul experienced forms of racism. Further, I explore how, for many in Seoul, the ways in which race and the construct of the foreigner created moments of utility and challenges of integration with new migrants moving to Seoul as a consequence of a globalizing Korea and the highly successful global marketing of Korean cultural products. For participants in Seattle, encounters with racism were pronounced and heavy among a predominantly White city and settler society. Threads of connections between these experiences are also explored as Seattle participants share their reflections on returning to South Korea and having to grapple with the hierarchies of race tied to skin color that exist locally.

Chapter 7 builds off the previous by articulating, through the narratives of participants, the structural connection between the US and South Korea that joins together the racial hierarchies and racialization processes of the two separate nation-states, serving to reinscribe Whiteness at its apex transnationally. Drawing from interest convergence theory articulated by critical race theorists, I argue that participants' propensity to only dating White foreigners is not just a racial preference. Rather, it is a consequence also of immigration policies that racially spatialize the foreigner population in Seoul. A racialized geography, I argue, demonstrates the connectedness between structural and interpersonal racism. A nuance can be read through the intimate reflection around sex and dating that participants shared with me on this journey, ultimately implicating many participants as both the racializer and the racialized, a position challenged by participants in many instances.

The conclusion chapter offers my reflections on how the development of this project, tied to my own lived experience and the connections I forged with many others over the years, helped me to understand the complexity of Korean gay life through the eyes of a diasporic Samoan. In the end, I hope that this book will succeed in telling a cross-cultural, transnational story, refracted through the lens of a Samoan researcher; a lens that I hope will offer dimension, not authority, and possibility around how my own complex positionality can open up more nuanced discussion of global and transnational queer mobilities.

Notes
1. In this manuscript, I use the official revised romanization of Korean adopted by the Korean government in 2000, as opposed to the McCune-Reischauer system favored in academia. I have chosen to do so because the revised romanization system better reflects the way my participants and I read, speak, and write in hangeul or Korean.
2. The Republic of Korea (ROK) is also known as South Korea. I use "Korea" and "South Korea" interchangeably throughout this book to refer to the Republic of Korea (South).
3. The *feāgaiga* is a sacred covenant, and in the Samoan context is often used to describe the relational responsibilities that

exist between brother and sister in Samoan culture. These responsibilities elevate the role of the sister as *tamasā*, or the exalted or sacred offspring – the term *sā* refers to something sacred in Samoan – as she has the power to bring life into this world. As such, a brother is meant to take care of her sister as well as protect and provide for her. The divinity in this framing also gives a sister the power to curse her brother and his children if he does not respect his role and play his part in upholding his duties in this relationship. As such, *feāgaiga* is a symbiotic relationality of protection, continuation of lineage, and respect. This engenders formality in many interactions between brother and sister as they are considered *sā* or *tāpū*. The *vā tapū*, or sacred space between brother and sister, is governed by the *feāgaiga*, thus, the critique is that a gender-neutral reading of *talanoa* is not something that can be achieved in the context of a woman researcher holding *talanoa* with participants who are men.

2

Sleepless in Seattle: The complex and complicated coming-out process

Powerful legacies: Barnabas and the Christian church

Behind one of Seattle's busiest suburban thoroughfares, a modernized two-part building sits nestled among pine trees. Boasting refreshed, yet somewhat dated decor, the shape and scale of the building is familiar to anyone who was raised in a Christian family; it clearly screams Church to everyone in the neighborhood. Flanked by massive car parks on either side, the need for the multitude of parking spaces became apparent once the *talanoa* began with one of the participants in my study.

> My mom's a deacon at that church. It's the largest Korean church in Seattle, with a congregation of more than 1500. She's been singing in the choir for years.

Barnabas,[4] a keen and eager participant, had moved to the US with his mother in 1980. He moved to Seattle in 1990 with his then partner, who is now his husband. Barnabas was much older than me, but he was full of energy and had a generous soul. He and his husband lived in a high-income neighborhood near downtown Seattle with their three children. Two of their children had been adopted, one had been conceived through surrogacy. We met on a cold and dreary Seattle Sunday in a café near the Seattle locks. I had taken the bus from my U-District base for 30 minutes to find him, having first connected through email.

Our *talanoa* took off quickly. We were eagerly sharing nearly immediately, and he peppered the conversations with requests about mine. He, like everyone else I would encounter on this journey, wondered what a Samoan kid from South Auckland was doing researching Korean gay men at a US university. I shared openly and genuinely but paid most attention to his story. A key focus of Barnabas' *talanoa* was on the importance of the Church, which played a part in bringing him and his husband together.

> I met my husband at a sleazy bar in Manhattan. At the time, my life revolved around family, God, and Jesus. When I met him, he was a Presbyterian boy from small-town Spokane. That night we talked for about two hours in this sleazy bar, and we talked about God. It was a Wednesday night, and I was 24, really energetic, [and] we talked about having a family. You know with other guys I met it was always, meet, sex, adios, but this other guy, it was different.

The connection between Barnabas and his husband had been initiated through the intertwining of their shared religious backgrounds. For Barnabas, these connections ran deeper than just meeting his future husband: his whole life had revolved around the Church. When he talked about the difficult decision he made to commit to a life with his husband and make the move to Seattle from New York to start a family, it was in the Church where they sought community.

> When we first moved to this neighborhood, we lived two blocks away from this Presbyterian Church. So, we decided to go one Sunday, and we sat at the back. I was holding both our babies and there was a tiny old Caucasian woman. She turned around and asked me how old my babies were. I told her that my youngest was barely three weeks old. And she turned around again. So, the whole congregation seemed OK, but I wasn't really buying into it at this point. After the service, my husband said to me: "Let's go back next week, I don't care what they say, I like building community." So, I said: "Sure, we'll come back." The next week when I came back, the woman had made our baby a quilt with her name on it. She said she had made a quilt for the past 35 years for every newborn baby in that congregation. She was single, never married, never had children, and had been attending the Church ever since it was established in 1965. So, it was really touching, and we have been going ever since.

The Pacific Northwest Native: Cain

Cain, another participant who had answered my call for participants, met with me on a rainy evening in south Seattle.[5] Cain was born and raised in Washington State, living in and around Seattle for most of their life. They left Seattle for college, and had spent time in South Korea since then, living in Seoul at roughly the same time

I had. These similarities in our stories were also tied to a similar politics we had around racial justice and a shared experience with Christianity and the church that Cain felt passionately about. For starters, Cain outlined how their family spent much time in their Korean church located in Kent, Washington. For Cain, their religious upbringing was important to how they came to understand their Korean identity in a country to which their parents had migrated in search of a more prosperous future.

> My parents were connected to a church since they first got to America, and I was baptized in that church. […] It was a place where we could be with people who look like me. We would eat Korean food, for example. I feel like there's another big thing about Christian churches in Seattle, where there's a loss of identity; where it can be White and mainstream.

This excerpt from our *talanoa* was explained carefully and deliberately by Cain. The struggles of growing up as a child of migrant parents added a different criticality to all decisions they made in life. These struggles would certainly cause them much strain when the issue of their divergent gender and sexual identity began to arise. But, in the initial stages of Cain's experiences growing up in the church, one of the primary issues was coming up against a mainstream that centered around Whiteness, which heightened the importance of attending a Korean American Christian Church. In response, Cain intimated that they had decided to participate in ancestor worship, common in Korean Confucian cultural praxis, to reclaim their identity.

> We never did ancestor worship, it's something I had to reclaim for myself recently. I put pictures of my

grandmothers in my room. My family completely adopted Christian rituals; it wasn't a picture of my grandparents hanging in our living room, it was a picture of Jesus. White Jesus, nonetheless.

Korean Protestants generally do not practice ancestor worship in a purely Confucian sense. Rather, they practice what is called *ch'uma*, or commemorative celebrations for departed family members. Cain supposed that reclaiming ancestor worship was an expression of their desire to resist the White textures of assimilationist pressures. Moreover, what was clear was that by contesting a Christian norm, they were reforming and reinvigorating a traditionally Confucian tradition associated with being Korean. But at heart of this remained the Church itself, as the referential and lens through which they were forced to refract their Korean identity.

Out of State: Azariah, Reuben, and Ezra

Azariah had been living in Seattle for eight years prior to our meeting. Our *talanoa* took place near the Space Needle, a Seattle landmark I had become familiar with. While Azariah was living with his fiancé in Seattle, where he finished law school and was practicing law, his story was situated within one of the largest Korean American communities in the US: Los Angeles. This would provide more depth and context to the stories I was encountering.

I grew up in a Presbyterian Church. Our family went every Sunday, and we ate lunch, like, every Sunday at the Church.

Azariah and Cain were the only participants who grew up in the US to inform me that they had attended Korean school, or *hagwon,* on the weekends.

But I mostly went for the free donuts.

"Understandable," I replied knowingly. Unlike Cain, Azariah recalled how Confucian norms were very much kept alive in their household by his mother, who would even drive out to his college, 40 miles away from his hometown, with *songpyeon* (rice cakes) just to celebrate *Seollal* and *Chuseok*[6] with him.

Reuben and Ezra were also born out of state but were also very much immersed in the KACC growing up. Reuben was a child from a mixed marriage: his father was White-American and his mother Korean. I was to learn that Reuben had been living in Korea at the same time I was. He found his fiancé in Seoul and returned to the US to marry him, choosing Seattle for its more open stance on queer rights and because Washington state had passed marriage equality legislation at the time. Reuben's maternal grandmother was the one who maintained a strong connection to the KACC in his hometown.

She only started attending Church when she got to America, funnily enough [...] I guess it was where she was able to feel connection and build her own sense of community.

Reuben touched on similar issues to Cain and Azariah in relation to their own personal faith. What Reuben's insights provided, further, was another clear link between the KACC and his maternal grandmother's integration into American society after migrating to the US. Ezra, who was the youngest participant in the study, provided an interesting counterpoint to Reuben's. Still, Ezra's story came to underscore the same theme of belonging and connectedness to the KACC that Reuben's grandmother appeared to be tapping into. This was important for Ezra, who expressed a disconnection from their Korean identity, being born to a Filipina mother. His link to Korea came through his father, who was adopted from an orphanage in Korea, and the complexity in his story was illustrated by the fact that, despite not being able to speak Korean, his father made the family attend Korean Church.

> I don't really claim my Korean side; the only thing Korean about me are my features. [...] Surprisingly, we always went to a Korean Church. Even though my dad doesn't speak any Korean. I don't speak any Korean either. And I've only ever been to the airport in Korea on my way to the Philippines.

Despite the language barrier, Ezra felt church was where he and his father could feel some connection to being Korean. Thus, the KACC was an important site of identity preservation, which became a prominent theme all participants in Seattle had mentioned. Ezra often felt like an outsider carrying mixed heritage. For him and his father, attending KACC services allowed them to feel a connection and create memories of a culture they had been estranged from. The complicated nature of Ezra's father's story has been mostly redacted at Ezra's request; however, his father's tale stories the intense complexities for Korean adoptees who were taken from Korea, severed from their cultural homes at a young age, and forced to face the reality of being a racial other in the US as they come of age.[7] As a Samoan raised in New Zealand, this was a story I could relate to, having grown up in Auckland where many Samoans attend one of our plentiful Samoan churches around the city. Churches also functioned as a place where Samoan culture, language, and heritage were practiced, maintained, and transmitted to the next generation. Many of my contemporaries still attend Samoan church services despite not being able to understand the language.

The complicated coming-out process

Azariah: "The first day she got to Seattle, I decided to tell her so that we would have the week. In my head, it sounded like a great idea [Azariah laughs]. It ended up being an incredibly awkward week. […] We agreed not to tell my dad, so she went back home, and I guess she was so physically and emotionally and visibly depressed, my dad asked about it and he found out the day she arrived. He booked a flight for the following weekend. […] He came with a stack of papers that he printed and there was this incredible article about: 'the problems of choosing to be gay.' It was put out by some organization that is along the lines of something like the 'Centre for Keeping Families Wholesome' or something."

Azariah's coming-out story was one of much turmoil and internal stress. For his family, the fact that Azariah was gay created a near existential religious crisis leading to what would be described by many as an attempt at conversion. Further to that, what

Azariah detailed was a story of strategy and complex calculation. His disclosure of his sexual identity clearly caused panic, but also caused his parents to seek for meaning among them. The strategizing on both their parts was about trying to figure out the best way to deal with Azariah's non-complicity with church teachings. The impact of the church in Azariah's story was further strengthened later in our *talanoa*, when he told me about the time he returned home for Thanksgiving after he had come out to his mother:

> I went home and found my mom had circled all these passages in the bible with Post-it Notes; I think it was to try and give her strength.

Azariah also detailed how his father reacted:

> Finding out that I didn't necessarily fit what his probable expectations were, for my future and having kids. He probably had so many questions, but he didn't really have a mechanism to ask those questions.

In both these responses, Azariah showed great generosity in framing his parents' reactions within one of confusion and fear. However, he also revealed that it was the church that provided them with comfort. When Azariah talks of his father not having a mechanism "to ask those questions," he is also making a statement about the lack of reference points in his father's life to any type of gay futurity. Read within a Korean familism lens and Korean historical perspective, where a Korean gay subjectivity cannot historically be seen, their reactions become situated, rather than just expressions of reactiveness to homosexuality that may be inferred from a straightforward heterosexist reading. Azariah also explained that he believed his father's reaction was part of a desire for him to have children and carry on the family name. This desire is a norm, in line with Confucian tradition that often centers patriarchal continuity of familial lines; a feature that Azariah would relay melded well with Christianity.

The interwoven nature of Confucian and Christian forces was also something demonstrated by Cain in their responses. Cain described how the interactional nature of Christianity and Confucian norms in their household affected their coming-out process.

Cain: I came out to my parents in 2014. This was after college, back at home, fed up with the idea of them not knowing who I was. It was really disastrous. I felt like what hurt them more was the fact that I stopped going to Church. That was more painful to my mom and dad. Many factors came together. The bible talks about not being gay for instance. So, there was definitely a hodgepodge of judgments placed on me at the same time. They thought I went to college in California and came back this heathen, a raging homosexual.

Patrick: Do you think, for your family, it was also to do with the expectations of a son in Korean culture?

Cain: Oh, yeah, the term filial piety. That was a big thing I was struggling with. Especially with being American, and that not being a prominent value; at least I don't see it as a prominent value. So, it's like: 'well you guys brought me to America, I'm just trying to be an individual, how this culture teaches me to be.'

Patrick: How do you feel about that? Do you feel like you should be allowed to integrate more with American culture/norms, versus holding onto Korean culture and its norms?

Cain: That's the gold question. I feel like American culture is problematic in a lot of ways. In terms of rejection of family, 18, you move out. I find a value in family ties; that's your original support network. It's also helped form my identity. That's a really important question, especially now because I ask myself: What is my duty to my family, my community, my Korean identity? But also, what is my duty to my queer family, to my queer brothers and sisters? How can we reconcile the two? Yeah, so those are the big questions, I don't have an answer for you.

The importance of family

The embeddedness of family and church is already well-telegraphed in participant stories, but the feeling of duty to family was something that also stood out as a major theme. Take this excerpt from Barnabas' narrative of how he made the choice to inform his mother of his decision to move away to Seattle.

I had a monetary motivation to help feed the family, in a way. I wanted to make things happen in America, make money, buy a penthouse, get a key for my mom. In the meantime, find someone to love. I wanted to please my family; the relationship among my sister, my mom, and me was so strong, we were inseparable. So, I wrote a 10-page letter to my mom. She's a 4th generation Presbyterian and we were so committed to church. I said to her in the letter that I wanted to take a chance to find my life somewhere besides New York. I folded it in parts and left $1,000 cash in her bedroom. Snuck it under her door and I left at four in the morning, on my birthday.

Barnabas' feelings of responsibility for his family when situated within Korean familism makes contextual sense, tying his own fortunes with theirs. His deep connection to his mother and sister was later explained within the context of the different roles his mother and father played in his life. His father immigrated to America ahead of him and his mother and as a result he developed a strong bond with his mother. Thus, the struggles of migrant pressure living in the US coalesced with the values and norms intrinsic to a Korean worldview. Throughout our *talanoa*, Barnabas explained how his mother had a strong reliance on him for both emotional and material support: a quality of their relationship that shows the traces of a uterine structure that helped to facilitate an affectionate aspect of their relationship. His choice of words, where he casts his family's story in the US as one of financial struggle in trying to "make it" in America, was one I understood as a Samoan whose mother had been motivated to move her entire family to New Zealand for very similar reasons. The power of Korean familial normative constructs was also evident in how he subsequently narrated this incident himself:

You know, for Asian, Korean families, unless there's a death, or some other pivotal moment, it's really hard to break that relationship. You know how Korean moms treat their sons, basically spoon feed them from birth. I think she cried for three months.

In this way, it can be said that, for Barnabas, the reluctance to come out to his mother was not necessarily a fear of rejection alone, which a heterosexist reading would infer as the main contributing factor. Rather, his fears were also related to the possibility that he may not be able to fulfil his role as a son within the family, immediately complicating this reading and individual calculus.

Cain explained that it was within the family unit that they were able to develop and appreciate a greater sense of their Korean ethnic heritage despite being born in America, heightening its importance to them and their lived reality.

> Yeah, family really helped to foster the aspect of my Korean identity that I still hold today. I'm really grateful for that. I've heard experiences of other Korean Americans where their parents shunned, completely rejected, their Korean identity. Like refusing to teach them the language, and "you should learn English." My parents were good at straddling that line between American and Korean culture. We always ate Korean food; my mom was and still is an amazing Korean cook. Really keeps our culture alive through the food, fermenting things, sent me to Korean school when I was young. We went to the biggest Korean church in Seattle.

Here Cain references life in a space that lays in the liminal, between two cultures; an existence that brings forth complexities juxtaposed further with a sexuality that goes against heteronormative structures prominent in both host and home countries. The term "straddling" that Cain chose demonstrates their awareness of the duality and complications of this intersectional experience; an experience that has family and church firmly placed in one camp as a migrant, whilst looking outward into an adopted homeland dominated by Whiteness and trying to navigate assimilationist structures. Thus, family, as the site where these forces all came together, became an important site for Cain to protect.

The importance of family and how it functioned as a support mechanism for participants was also demonstrated in Reuben's story of coming out to his mother. His was a staggered process, in which he told his sister first, followed by his father, and finally his mother.

> My mom was the most emotionally affected by it. She cried when I came out to her, she was pretty upset; she was more worried about me, she felt sorry for me. […] She was sad for the life that I would have, that it would be hard for me, or she was sad for the fact that my life had been hard up to that point, harder than a straight person.

Reuben's *talanoa* helped to highlight the interrelated connections between participants and family members and how they work in reciprocal ways. All participants described a process wherein all family members were intersubjectively constructing their own sense of self with participants in many ways. Here, Reuben's mother was distraught, but according to Reuben it was not because she felt her son had violated the religious norms of her family's values system; rather, he interprets it as a mother's instinct to protect her son, showing through in her emotional response. In reference to the concept of uterine families (Wolf, 1972), her instinct to protect her son was perhaps connected to her own marginality as a racial other in the US. As a Korean mother, her desire to protect her son is part of her identity and sense of personhood. The opportunity to realize this has been denied to her by the existence of a sexual identity, embodied and lived by her son, that is marginalized by society. This nuance could easily be framed as homophobia, but clearly Reuben's mother's concern here is not simply that her son is gay, but rather that she has not been able to protect him as much as she has felt obliged to as part of who she is as a Korean mother. As such, I read this as a critique of the inherent violence that heterosexist structures impart on bodies and desires that contradict the rigidity of a heteronormative matrix. This again, when read within the specific Korean familism context where social welfare has fallen directly on the family unit itself, which includes social, economic, and emotional support, shows the complications involved in deciding to come out for Korean gay men, moving just the confines of a closet.

Constructing narratives of convenience

Barnabas: When my mother found out that my husband was more than just my roommate, she broke down in tears. It was hard for me to tell her; you know what it's like […]. So, she tells everyone in the Church that he's my roommate and together we support and adopt kids who are needy.

This conveniently imaginative narrative was something that Barnabas advised me he complied with. He did so because it gave his mother the opportunity to preserve her position within the KACC. I was to learn that this was important to both him and his mother, as she ran a dry-cleaning business in Seattle's suburbs, serving predominantly Korean clients. Barnabas explained that, in his experience, he often found the KACC was an important site for economic exchanges that helped to establish Korean businesses through community patronage. In fact, all Seattle participants agreed that the church was an important site where these connections were made, which is significant as Korean American studies literature documents the way crucial Korean American business links often are sustained within Korean American communities in the US (Park, 1997).

Narratives of convenience were also negotiated and deployed in situations that required interacting with extended family members. This often necessitated having other members of the immediate family enact roles of strategic deception. When Barnabas took his family to South Korea during the summer, his husband stayed behind, but his children and mother went with him.

> Everyone on my mother's side has passed away except her eldest. All her cousins came to see us. So, my eldest (adopted Chinese heritage), he's a good-looking kid, and everyone was like, "Oh he's the Park," he instantly gets $100. [...] They said to me, "oh your wife must be White." [...] I didn't say anything, but my mom said, "yeah, she's working at home." [...] The relatives said, "she's a good wife." My kids didn't know what was going on, although

my redhead calls me mummy; the relatives didn't really understand what she meant by that.

In this interaction, I read Barnabas' complicity in this deception as an expression of his care for his mother. He allowed his mother to construct a narrative that conveniently left out specifics to protect her position and prestige within the family. In our subsequent conversations, he confirmed that he was silent because he knew that his coming out would affect how the extended family would view her. At this stage of his life, if his extended family found out about his sexuality, he would not be directly impacted in any material way, as he had his own secure and prosperous family in Seattle with his husband. His mother, however, was now a widow, far more embedded within the family and community network. By remaining silent as she built this narrative of convenience, he was in many ways performing his duty as a Korean son to also protect his mother.

Coincidentally, this narrative of convenience was also something that Azariah experienced when he traveled with his fiancé to South Korea, also during the same summer.

> Before we travelled, we sat down and talked about how we would be introduced and who we would be introduced to. It was decided that we would just be introduced as chingu [friends]. [...] When I came out there was an understanding that I would not be coming out to anyone in my extended family. Over the years, my mom's side all know now, but my dad's side, still nobody knows.

Azariah also detailed in our *talanoa* the reason why his father's side was kept in the dark. For Azariah, it was to ensure peaceful relations were maintained between his father and the rest of his relatives.

> They're extremely judgmental people, my father feels a
> lot of pressure from them.

Azariah's father was the only son of four siblings. Azariah explained how loyal his father was to his family, despite them being "cold, minimalist, and conservative Korean." When Azariah had been forced out by his mother's disclosure to his father, his father was devastated but never thought about disowning him. Azariah explained that when his father had the "talk" with him after his "accidental" coming-out, his father had said to him: "The most important thing is family." This intimated that, although existing explanations posit that many Korean families are intensely conservative and religious, which can read as heterosexist and homophobic, the strength of the bonds forged in the Korean family can also manifest protective responses. Despite disappointment occurring – which Azariah also storied as part of his father's reaction – the Korean family can adapt and ultimately strategize.

For Azariah, this had positive effects. He said that the gradual way that his relationship was introduced into the familial structure allowed for people in his extended family to slowly make the connection themselves. By using a narrative of convenience, it allowed him and his partner to expose themselves to the family as non-threatening and gave his extended family time to get used to seeing them together. And although he is yet to come out officially, he believes most people "kind of knew" or put two and two together.

On my mom's side, he still got introduced with the words chingu, but I think everyone knew what that meant. I don't think anyone was comfortable saying namja chingu [boyfriend]. I think that is maybe too much. But everyone seemed fine meeting him. […] It was amazing when the two of us stayed at my grandmas, my mom's mom's place, for a couple nights. My grandma doesn't speak a ton of English. She spoke what little she knew to him and then she told me: "You look very 환해Not converting properly. [shiny] and I've never seen you this bright and happy." Yeah, and I think that went amazingly well. The rest of my mom's extended family, I think everybody's OK. There was nothing special about it. Nothing particularly different than meeting another friend, but I think everyone knew and didn't act weird about it, which I think is amazing.

Azariah's experience was important as it demonstrated how a narrative of convenience can help to smooth possible tensions within a familial setting if deployed with a contextual sensitivity. If he had pushed a messaging and approach that asserted a gay identity in which has family had to simply comply, it may have caused unmanageable tension, which could have impacted his parents in negative ways.

For Reuben, a narrative of convenience was set up to protect his Korean grandmother, who connected him to his Korean side. When he came out to his mother, as quoted earlier, her reaction was very emotional. But later he assured me that she was at peace with it. When we talked about his grandmother, who he called a "third parent," he said he would never tell her: a decision that his parents also agreed to.

> She was typical in the sense of a lot of Korean immigrants. They needed a community to get help from, and the church is that for the Korean American community.

Thus, Reuben's decision not to tell her protected her from having to experience any form of dislocation from this community as a result of the predominance of heterosexist attitudes. This is, once again, demonstrating that for Korean gay men, the context of coming out can be a far more complicated process than merely synthesizing a homosexual self with other parts of their personhood. Namely, participants understood that it requires more careful consideration of familial context and the impact it has on all members of the family. When all the factors discussed in this chapter come together – migration pressures, integration, church, family, and integrity – the use of a narrative of convenience, I believe, is an adaptive tool that bears the hallmarks of nuanced strategizing that complicates our ideas of what coming out looks like.

Discussion questions

What does the conceptualization of a *narrative of convenience* offer our understanding of the coming-out process for gay men of different cultures within your society?

Considering some of the complicated factors that impact the lives of Korean gay men in Seattle, briefly detailed here, what are the variables or forces that mediate decisions you make around how you describe your sexuality to others?

How does an intersectional lens help us to complicate discussions around heterosexism and homophobia and its impact on coming out for gay men in the context offered here?

What space do you think there is for *narratives of convenience* in the way you understand the importance of sexual visibility and visibility politics in your society?

As this book and chapter focuses on gay men, how different or similar do you think the stories offered here would be in relation to the stories of gay or queer women?

Notes

4. All participant names have been changed to aliases for confidentiality.

5. Since this research was conducted, Cain has stated that they are non-binary and goes by they/them pronouns.

6. *Seollal* is also known as Lunar New Year in Korea; *Chuseok* is also known as the Thanksgiving Harvest, commonly referred to as Korean Thanksgiving. On both occasions, Koreans usually visit their hometowns to pay respect to their ancestors. The specific ancestor worship ceremony, a Confucian practice, is known as *Chesa*.

7. Much literature exists on the experiences of exclusion and the adaptive strategies for Korean adoptees as returnees to Korea and their experiences in the US. See Eleana Kim's (2010) *Adopted Territory* for a comprehensive overview of how Korean adult adoptees negotiate and create notions of kinship and cultural transnational citizenship.

3

Doing the transnational time warp: Constructing difference between Korean America and contemporary South Korea

Something I noticed early on through *talanoa* was that many of the participants in Seattle often said, unequivocally, that they did not like to hang out with other Koreans. This was almost entirely the case for the men who had recently (within a decade) moved to Seattle. Their feelings were very strong on the issue and, at first, I put it down to the heterogeneity that is found within all cultures and thought very little of it. But as *talanoa* progressed, I began to sense that this tension was more than just divergence in opinion and experience. Rather, this tension spoke to experiences and understandings of being Korean, differentiated by location and context, transnationally and precariously tied (rather loosely) together by a common ethnic/cultural identity, language, and history. The complex reality in which participants moved and engaged with their culture across a vast ocean offers all of us complex questions around diaspora and host/home essentialisms of identity, underscoring the role both geographic as well as temporal nodes of connection can play for ethnically bordered community.

In this chapter, I trace participant narratives to illuminate how the differences between Korean America and contemporary South Korea can be comprehended through the way Seattle participants articulated their experiences and unfamiliarities with certain practices within the Korean American community in Seattle. Namely, despite all participants claiming their Korean heritage as an important lens to their construction of identity, their understanding of what Korean identity meant in the Seattle context differed depending on their experiences of growing up in South Korea for some and being raised in Seattle for others. Consequently, complexity around the way the Korean American community in Seattle impacted sexual visibility for many participants is added.

Through this chapter, I theorize how these contexts are temporally bound, refracting, and diverging participants' engagement with "Koreanness" or Korean identity. Those raised primarily in South Korea found themselves encountering a Korean American community that they storied as being stuck in a conservative South Korean past. As was detailed in the introduction, Korean migration from South Korea has a long history in the US, with the 1950s and 1960s representing pivotal moments facilitating the establishment of vibrant and studious Korean American communities in the continental US. Due to this temporal node of establishment, participants believed the foundations of the Korean American community was not only religious, but also static. In doing so, they offered a fuller understanding of the social shifts that South Korea had undergone since the 1990s and its intentional drive toward globalization. This, in their own words, left behind a Korean America still anchored to a migrant past.

Structures/discourses of exclusion and forms of resistance

Samson had spent most of his life in South Korea and migrated to the US with his now husband in his late 20s. Like Reuben and his partner in the previous chapter, Samson had come to the US firstly to be able to marry, and secondly to be able to work in a space he felt would free them from the overtly patriarchal nature and toxic masculinity of Korean working life. Samson had worked for a major conglomerate in South Korea, among what he characterized as typical conservative Korean men constantly harassing him about his life and plans for starting his own family. When Samson moved to Seattle, however, he encountered a Korean American community that seemed steeped in structures and norms that were from another time. Namely, the intensely Christian character of the Korean community in Seattle was particularly off-putting, especially given the aspirations he had for moving to the US in the first place. In fact, Samson even said he wished not to have any Korean friends in Seattle at all.

> I don't want to have any Korean friends here, they're too Christian for me, and more conservative than Koreans in Korea. I'm actually worried about them finding out

and talking about me, he [another participant] is the only Korean friend I have.

The fact that Samson had only one Korean friend in Seattle despite the large Korean population was an important aspect of his responses. As a child of a migrant family myself, I knew how important it was to my mother to find social support from her ethnic community when she moved. Moreover, one feature of *talanoa* with other participants, as well as prior literature, advances the notion that the Korean American community was often an important source of social support and networks for new migrants. The fact that Samson chose to reject the Korean American community as a possible support network clearly speaks to the complicated calculation he had to make for his own safety, the reason being the perceived conservative and religious nature of Korean Americans in Seattle. His worry was that he would be outed to the wider community by another Korean.

> Recently, I met two people [Koreans]; one was a married woman, the other was a married guy. They were saying how they were scared about their kids growing up in the US because of a lot of drug problems and of how there are a lot of gay teachers. They specifically focused on that; they obviously didn't know I was gay, but that's what they were worried about.

The deeply heterosexist and Christian-infused basis that helped to shape some of the commonly held images of the Korean American community is well documented in Korean American studies, as part of Asian American gay and lesbian literature (Bong, 2008; Cho and Sohn, 2016; Henry, 2020; Kim and Hahn,

2006; ; Lim and Johnson, 2001; Seo, 2001; Thomsen, 2019; Um, Kim, and Kim, 2016). However, its effects on Korean gay men recently migrated to the US have been relatively understudied.

Samson's position on the Korean American community – that it was more conservative and Christian than what he was used to in Korea proper before migrating – was not unique to him. The participants I spoke to who had recently migrated to Seattle all showed a type of marginality that excluded them from feeling safe in participating actively within the Korean American community. Interestingly, this disconnection was not something that they felt any sense of regret over. Rather than framing this experience as a function of exclusion that made them feel disconnected and any type of mental distress, they relayed a sense of relief to be able to disconnect from these conservative structures. This disconnection often came in the form of living a more open life in the workplace. In this excerpt, Samson explains how he came out to his boss in Seattle and how he felt a new sense of freedom in being able to do so.

> When I got a job, because my spouse wasn't working, we needed health insurance. So, I told my boss I was gay. He said: "Thank you for saying that, but you didn't have to tell me, here it doesn't really matter, this will be the best place for you guys." Even his kids went to school where there are gay parents, and his kid was a high school student at the time. So, "if you guys want to have a family, you can adopt or have a surrogate child." It was big for me, because in Korea I was working in a really masculine industry and if they found out about me, I would have had to quit my job.

Samson's experience as evidenced by this excerpt suggested that within Seattle and the US, there may exist two worlds for Korean gay men: a Korean one and an American one. This means that for Korean gay men who migrate to the US in search of a more open queer life, like Longres (1996) concluded in their work, the act of coming out is complicated by navigating these worlds. It also suggests that the Korean American community – which represents and defines how Americans engage with Korean people, culture, and history in the US – is likely to be seen as deeply religious and conservative on queer issues. For people like Samson, it meant adapting to the coming-out process much like other participants in the previous chapter who were raised in Seattle, albeit from different criticalities. The participants navigated these exclusionary structures as a product of being raised within them, as diasporic Koreans. Samson and others born in South Korea were developing a transnational subjectivity, differentiating their experiences from a diasporic lens. In this sense, there were exercising a form of simultaneous embeddedness (Yeoh, Willis, and Fakhri, 2003), drawing references to frame their experiences within both contemporary South Korean society and modern day America concurrently. This meant not only navigating living in American society, but also navigating Korean American society at the same time, which marks their stories out as distinct and different.

Around the issue of coming out and visibility, Samson believed there was no need to come out to extended family whilst living away from them in the US, and it also meant there was no need to be "visibly gay" in Korean American spaces. Narratives like Samson's suggest that participants who were exercising a transnational subjectivity did not feel it necessary to engage in contemporary Korean American spaces; they were lifting their connections beyond a diasporic community, with the distance between Seoul and Seattle allowing them to live in separate worlds at the same time. By contrast, there was a reactiveness to Korean American spaces, forged when diaspora subjectivities they were encountering (in their minds) were dated in their ideologies and conservative in their foundations.

This idea was mirrored by YG, another participant who had just migrated to Seattle when we met. YG was out to his workmates and even marched in Seattle Pride as part of his workplace's participation in the annual event. He was a lively character, who by sheer coincidence moved into an apartment four doors down from mine. He jokingly referred to himself as a racist who only dated Koreans. He had, according to himself, cultivated a sense of pride in his gay identity, which did not seem to be bringing him any tension regarding his Korean heritage. I would later run into him again at Seoul Pride following the parade at a café in Itaewon, full of life and happy to be among his many Korean queer friends in Seoul at the 2017 iteration of the festival.

He openly declared himself as the most "out" among his Korean gay friends in Seattle (none of whom he succeeded in convincing to participate in the study). What was interesting about YG is that he was an active participant in gay clubs and activist movements in Korea, and yet, in Korea, was not open about his sexuality to anyone besides fellow "sisters" in Seoul.

This "sisters" terminology had two contemporary common uses in Seoul, in my experience. The first was inclusive naming that helped to denote a shared sexual identity. The second was as a term, used among some gay Korean activists, that can be likened to "comrade" in certain contexts[8]. YG would often refer to me as his "sis" in our conversations. He was also fascinated and somewhat relieved that a person from an ethnic minority, who had spent so much time living in Korea and could speak Korean well, was conducting this research. We had shared reference points for Korean gay life and were roughly the same age; we both recalled watching Seoul Pride grow from meager beginnings in 2009, ultimately exploding as a popular event for hundreds of thousands of Koreans toward the end of my doctoral research in 2018.

For YG, living in Seattle presented two Americas. The first was one in which gay people were free to live open lives that he felt impressed by. The second was a Korean America that was intensely conservative and exclusionary, and which led to him, much like Samson, distancing himself.

> **Patrick:** What were your views of American society in terms of acceptance of homosexuality versus that of Korea, and what's your experience been like since you got here?
>
> **YG:** I was surprised to see that many homosexuals – and gays in general, even other queer identities – are open here and open themselves up to society. I even see rainbow flags in their homes. In fitness centers, I see signs where they invite sexual diversity, and people are so open with sexuality in general here. This is interesting.
>
> **Patrick:** So, do you think that means you can be more open here with your sexual identity?

YG: That's a difficult question actually. Even though American society is more open to it, the Korean community is very conservative. [...] Even though I haven't been here that long, I don't go to a Korean church, which is the largest Korean community in America, as I'm not Christian.

YG's migration to the US was for work purposes; he was highly educated and was pursuing work in Seattle after completing his doctorate in South Korea. This makes YG's travel to the US the case of a highly skilled worker exercising educational credentials to facilitate his transnational mobility, and his contribution should be read within this context. However, it does offer us more insights into the complex way Korean gay men recently arrived from South Korea were engaging with the Korean American community and spaces they had ethnic kinship ties toward.

Resisting the time warp in Korean America

I was referred to participant Jacob through another participant. Jacob was also married to an American citizen and had also moved to Seattle for work purposes. Jacob had no desire to make Korean friends in Seattle either, citing the insular nature of Koreans in the US.

No, I don't want to make more Korean friends because they make me uncomfortable. First of all, the community is very small and Korean people are usually very different from Westerners. They always want to be in a group; even if I want to do something on my own, I have to do it with them. I did that in Korea, and I don't want to do that in the US. You know, Koreans always hanging out together. Especially the Korean community in Seattle, they just hang out with each other, and they don't hang out with people from different cultures.

Jacob's disavowal of what he described as a typology associated with Korean forms of socializing is interesting because he rejects a group formation in favor of one that is more individual. In this way, he can be seen to be choosing to embrace a more individualistic discursive strand in his own behavior, as opposed to a more collective strand in the behavior of Korean Americans. His comments on the insularity of Koreans in Seattle certainly sit comfortably with other comments that YG made. Of course, this is not to suggest singularity in how Koreans understand their own culture and experiences. Rather, it functions as a reminder of the divergence of engagement with cultural ideas and norms that operate at an individual level in differentiated ways.

Ezekiel, another participant who was born in Korea, was to relay in similar terms what Samson, YG, and Jacob had all stated regarding this somewhat fixed shaping and foundation of Korean American cultural norms and practices that seemed rooted in the past and connected to the big movement of Koreans to the US following the Korean War. In contrast to Jacob's, YG's, and Samson's disavowal, Ezekiel mostly only spent time with Koreans. He had moved to Seattle for university and was near graduation when we met. This excerpt is from a follow-up conversation we had in Seoul after Ezekiel had moved back following his graduation.

Ezekiel: I mostly stayed around Koreans in Seattle; it was easy to hang out with them because you know we're all Korean. And I didn't know anyone that was there at the time.

Patrick: Was it your experience that most Koreans in the Korean American community tended to socialize together and not really mix with people from other ethnic backgrounds?

Ezekiel: Yeah, my group of friends mostly just stuck with Koreans because it was easiest. We all spoke the same language; we all understood each other because we have the same culture. You know, American culture is different from Korean culture. So, we mostly hang out with each other.

Patrick: Did that mean you also went to Church? As I know that the Korean American community in Seattle is quite Christian.

Ezekiel: I didn't go to Church with them but it's very Christian and very conservative there. But that's how Koreans are in America in general, I think.

The gulf between the Korean American world and an American world was real to participants and they were deliberately constructing a demarcated boundary between the two in our *talanoa*. The Korean American world was conjured up by participants as one that is conservative and Christian; the American world, in contrast, was progressive and more likely to afford sexual freedoms. Participants also theorized, in their own way, why this was the case. YG explained it as a type of temporal-dependent social construct, where the Korean American community had been built around structures that formed in a specific time and space:

For many of them, they moved here in the 60s and
70s when Korea was really conservative. So, they've
maintained their conservative ways, and Korea has
moved on.

He clarified this position by indicating that he was referring to
the way that gay life in Korea had moved on, in the sense that his
gay life in Korea was much better than it was in the US.

The night life in Korea is much better than here […] for
me. I also prefer to date Korean guys so it's not so great
for me here.

Interestingly, the US being a place of freedom and a better
queer life was the type of chatter I had heard from my own ex-
boyfriend and among circles in Seoul I was familiar with. What
YG's experience suggests is that, because they had experience of
the Korean American community being stuck in a time-warp of
sorts, and because in Seattle not many Korean gay men existed
in queer spaces, it was not a great life for him. He was not the
only participant that spoke of this transnational diasporic time
warp. Jacob made this observation in eerily similar terms to YG:

Most of the Korean Americans I know, their parents
moved here a long time ago when Korea was still really
conservative. They have the same idea of their parents
about Korean culture and life. So, it's like Korean society
has changed a lot, but Korean Americans have not.

This may appear a peculiar observation to make considering that
none of the participants born in Korea had disclosed their sexual
identity beyond their circle of gay friends in Korea. None of them
had disclosed their sexual identity to anyone in their family either.

But disclosure is only considered a necessary part of gay identity synthesis in developmental models advanced by psycho-social models like the Cass model. When read in reference to wider social changes that have been carefully traced by scholars like Campbell (2016) and Abelmann (2013) in South Korea, it makes contextual sense. These scholars posit that a new type of neoliberal self-cultivation discourse has emerged among Korea's rising generation that emphasizes the act of creating a future on your own. This emerging shift brings situatedness and context to the temporal divide identified by participants in Seattle. South Korean families, and civil society in particular, have undergone many structural changes over the past six decades specifically, as discussed in the introduction through various Korean familism lenses. With the rapid advancements in technological links across the globe, this process promises even more transnational possibilities and divergences that participants in Seattle were foreshadowing in our *talanoa*.

On being raised in and choosing Korean America

Other examples of emerging divergences abound in the narratives of participants, including some of those who were born in the US. This divergence in narratives is especially pertinent when we bring a racialized lens into the circulating discourses that are affecting the way the participants construct interpretations of their own lived experiences. Perhaps most telling is when Cain narrates the difficulties they faced when seeking help from an American therapist while trying to navigate the coming-out process and disclosure to their parents. Cain relayed in our *talanoa* how they were struggling with trying to negotiate the pressures of family and resolve their understanding of their sexual identity by visiting a White therapist.

> I've been trying to see therapists lately, and it's with this White lady at the moment, and after I've been telling her about what I'm going through, her response was simple: "why don't you move out?" I wanted to scream at her, "lady I'm Korean, It's not that easy!"

Cain was referring to the complexities that their identity formation processes were subjected to; processes that all participants who were born in the US had alluded to in our *talanoa*. Their sense of identity as Koreans in the US was constructed mutually through or in reference to/against the KACC and through familial values imbued with Confucian values that emphasized familial continuity and that presented as heterosexist. It was this complexity that meant that they had to navigate sexual visibility with more nuance than just "coming out of the gay closet."

This complexity is most evident in this excerpt from Ezekial's *talanoa* about why he continued to stay connected with his group of Korean American friends despite understanding how intensely heterosexist their views toward gay people were.

Ezekial: Lots of them go to church and churches are supposedly conservative. So, one of my friends actually mentioned that once when we were at a café drinking coffee. There was a gay couple walking next to us. My friend said, "I would never ever understand those guys." She was Christian and was very conservative. She said that all her friends think the same way. So, I was thinking I would never be able to come out to them.

Patrick: So, despite this experience, what do you think continued to draw you to hanging out with them? Was it because you felt connected to them as Korean?

Ezekial: I understand them. It's their right not to like us. I don't care about that. The reason why we became friends is that we had something that connects us. Being Korean.

Patrick: A lot of people I've spoken to have said that Koreans in America are more conservative than Koreans in Korea. This is interesting because America is supposed to be less conservative.

Ezekial: It's not just Seattle Koreans though. I think it's because a lot of Koreans moved to America in the 70s and 80s when Korea was super conservative, and their thoughts still remain. But Korea has changed but they didn't change.

Although Ezekial homed in on a different time period than the one chosen by Jacob and YG, the theme of the Korean American community, in the participants' experiences, being based on a dated version of Korean society came through, despite the differences in their ages and experiences. But further to that, what Ezekial stories here is something I understood well. As a gay man with experiences of converging marginalizations, being gay matters, and navigating this space is extremely complicated and can be distressing, but it is not the *only* thing that matters. This complexity requires you to think specifically about the best options for navigating the particularities of your ethnic community in relation to your gay subjectivity.

Linear coming-out models like the Cass Model (1979) and the Troiden Model (1989) are very useful tools in helping us to understand the likelihood of experiencing distress whilst working through our own gay subjectivities, but what the Cass Model and other linear models like it argue – that disclosure should become a non-issue once you have resolved your homosexual identity with other parts of the self – cannot account for this context fully. To Cass' credit, in later iterations of their work, they acknowledged the inability of their own model to account for cultural difference. What this reminds us, however, is that for Korean gay men in Seattle, who occupy an intersectional space where intersecting forms of marginalization are embedded in their experience, two parts of the self are fundamentally structured by different normative, cultural, geographic, and temporal spaces, suggesting that *holding*, rather than resolving, tensions may be another framework in which we can understand the complexity of culturally embedded notions and discussions around sexual visibility.

Considering these complexities, I argued in the previous chapter that participants, especially those that were born in the US, navigated these complexities by bringing family with them through narratives of convenience designed to keep harmony for their family inside and outside the home. Ezekial's example shows that embodying a subjecthood forged through converging experiences of marginalization can force one to stay closeted in order to access social support from an ethnic community, despite its intensely heterosexist character. This layered conflict was especially pronounced for Ezekial as they had only moved to the US specifically for university studies. As a racialized other (to be explored further in subsequent chapters) trying to navigate a gay Seattle that other participants were to story as racist, it makes sense that he sought to strengthen his Korean networks instead. As a Samoan in New Zealand, I often have faced a similar decision: whether I should ignore the heterosexist conservative textures of the Samoan community in participating fully or gravitate toward a queer community that can often lack racial reflexivity.

Discussion questions

What are some other concepts and terms that we can use to theorize what has been referred to here as a transnational time warp?

Is there a difference between a diasporic positionality in the sexuality context and a transnational positionality, and how do these operate in the context covered here?

Can you think of other examples that relate to how stories of migration can shift the way that we know and remember our own cultures?

What are your thoughts regarding having to compromise one part of yourself (sexuality) to protect another part of yourself (culture), as was detailed by Ezekial in this chapter?

Diary entry

June 10th, 2017.

10:14 am Pacific Standard Time at SeaTac International Airport.

America, it's been fun (and very not fun), but it's time to go back "home."

To where my "Seoul" has been for nearly a decade.

To where this journey all began.

I'm so excited to be going back to Korea, a place where I feel so much more at home in than America ever could. Can't wait to trade the Space Needle for Seoul Tower and to run up Namsan's sides during the spring and fall.

Peace out Seattle.

Note

8.   In Taiwan, the term *Tongzhi*, or comrade, is often used among queer activists as a marker of shared identity (see Wang et al., 2009). In many ways, this was deployed in a similar, yet more jestful, way among Korean gay men I came across in the activist arena. In Korea, the common terms *ŏnni* or *unni* are used by younger women; she refers to an older woman in her social and familial circle as *unni* as a sign of social and genealogical kinship. Men use the term *hyung,* or "older brother," to express the same relationality. The term *unni* has been said to have once been used among men as well.

4

Global Korean gaze: Influences from the "West" and the emergence of a Korean gay consciousness in Seoul

Hank: Lots of things I know about from overseas are through the media because I haven't been to many countries. I have only been to England, Japan, and China. So, I guess obviously, the main thing is our country is conservative, which caused not many people to come out.

Patrick: Do you think that is changing and it's easier for people to come out now?

Hank: I think so. I wouldn't say it's a lot easier than five or six years ago. It is changing but the difference between the past five years and now is very small.

But the social atmosphere and acceptance is a lot more different from back then. The speed for change is accelerating forward.

Patrick: What makes you optimistic about it?

Hank: Because of everything I've seen from LGBT activists and reformers. In the center of everything, I see everything. Events, shows, and protests. I witness and hear about everything. Because this year's [2017] queer protest was the biggest I have ever seen it.

Patrick: Yes, they said it was 85,000 people. How does that compare to your experience from previous ones?

Hank: My prior experience was in 2011 at Chongno. There were only 2,000 or couple thousands of people. Then the next year, it was 4,000 to 5,000 people. Then the next year was at Hongdae, 2013, that was 15,000. The next year was 20 something thousand. In 2015, it moved to Seoul City Hall and there were 30,000 people. Last year it was 50,000 and this year 85,000.

When I departed Seattle in 2017, nearly a decade had passed since I first landed in South Korea, and the assertive change in queer environments, confidence, and formation of communities in Seoul was palpable to me. When I first attended Seoul Pride in 2009, it was a small procession of fewer than a couple of hundred participants, stared down by many Korean shoppers in the Sinchon district, upset at the way the parade created people movement and traffic inconveniences. In 2018, when I wrapped up fieldwork, it was estimated 120,000 people had attended the

Seoul Queer Culture Festival, including myself. A change in the way Koreans were talking about sexual minorities and the queer community was clearly in the air. LGBT rights even became the subject of heated and typically misguided discussion for the very first time during an election campaign (2017 and again in 2022) as presidential hopefuls on the Korean left brought LGBTQI+ issues into national debates. This was a major event for many of us who had lived through multiple failed attempts to pass comprehensive anti-discrimination laws for all people living in Korea; attempts that failed due to intense pushback from conservative Christian groups because the human rights activists insisted that LGBTQI+ minorities be covered by the legislation.

I also "fondly" recall the way an elementary school student I taught in Geoje-do, an island off the coast of the Gyeongsangnam district, told me in no uncertain terms that there were no gays in Korea. Although a confronting experience for a young queer who had just become brave enough to sit in their own gay skin, these kinds of encounters presented my first real foray into the murky waters that sit opaquely between sexual identity and sexual practices. I was eventually able to understand that this encounter and many others like it I was to have in my time in Korea were symptoms of shifts in understanding around sexuality in South Korea that were yoked to the forces of modernity and Western influences. In many ways, the gay identity we claim and know in Western contexts bore no congruency on how gay practices of sexual desire and intimacy were documented in the Korean historical record (Bong, 2008).

Prior to South Korea's integration into the global community, to practice homosexuality often meant restricting sexual acts between two men to weekend liaisons, facilitated in counter-public practices and in spaces such as parks, bars, and clubs camouflaged within the public domain and only understood by gay men and queers who understood the hidden, discursive code.[9] Song Pae Cho (2011) detailed the hidden practices of gay life in Korea in their study and what they termed the "rise of the bats." Moreover, Korean norms of homosociality (men socializing only with other men, women with other women) often allowed for the practice of homosexuality to exist and be tolerated if it was never given a social identity outside the gender binary and heterosexual family (Lee, 2016). This erasive practice functioned in normality for many years as South Korea maintained its hermit position to the outside world. But with the social and political environment shifting as South Korea emerged as a democracy in 1987, and the subsequent implementation of the *Seghyewa* policy of Global Korea in the 1990s, a desire for cosmopolitan credentials meant that a desire for a gay or queer social identity in South Korea rose in line with Korea's opening to the rest of the world.

In Asia more broadly, many scholars have argued against the universality of a cosmopolitan gay identity in critiquing the colonial assumptions infused in the spread of global gay and queer discourses. Petrus Liu (2007) warns us that emerging gay subjectivities and epistemes of desire in Asia should be seen as a product of the impact of democratization and globalization. Jackson and colleagues (2013) add that the opposition toward homosexuality in Asia is more likely to be a product of the threat it poses to traditional familial structures than a product of homophobia. However, South Korea's militant fundamentalist

Christian bloc complicates the Korean situation further. Inderpal Grewal and Caren Kaplan (2001) mention how some scholars have pointed out that the rhetoric of diversity and globality with respect to sexual identity produces "monumentalist gay identities" which can elide radical sexual difference.

The connections, effects, and flows of Western discourses, cultural productions, and ideas

Martin: Maybe Korean society follows some sort of global standard. I think that Sex and the City helped us a lot. Because many girls thought after watching the show: "there are gay people," because they watched the show and after the popularity of Sex and the City, there are gay guys in society.

The power of media to change people's perceptions around social formations and discourses is robustly debated in media studies literature (see Ball-Rokeach and DeFleur, 1976 for a review). Indeed, many participants held the belief that Western discourses that were circulated by media formats that proliferated and intensified in the 1990s having a real effect in shaping both activist movements and their sense of an emerging gay self. When I met Martin, who was a well-known activist running Seoul's first ever shelter for queer youth, he intimated this idea to me strongly. The day our *talanoa* took place, he had just attended a Church service at one of Seoul's few Christian congregations that welcomed sexual minorities. This church was run by a White pastor from the US. Martin had been raised Christian, more specifically Catholic, like I had. He was also from what he termed a low-income background. The parallels between our stories provided for a lively and lengthy *talanoa* in which he shared a lot of intimate details. One story included his own experience of praying dutifully to the Christian God to change him; when God failed to respond, he finally concluded that there must be nothing wrong about being gay because God had not turned him straight.

The specific constructed history of gay activism in Western societies was useful in Martin's line of work. He felt that queer activism in Western societies helped to also bring to light the struggles of Korea's own sexual minority community in inspiring others to action as a type of political strategy. He said it helped to highlight the shortcomings of South Korea's government on the international stage. This strategy drew on a type of international modelling that has been examined closely in international relations theory about international law and about state socialization and its ability to engender domestic policy changes within a community of likeminded liberal nations (Acharya, 2004; Ayoub, 2015; Cortell and Davis, 1996; Friedman, 2012; Goodman and Jinks, 2004; Guzman, 2008; Slaughter, 1995).

> Inspiration is a big part; when I was in the UK, I visited some local gay support centers for youth. I realized, wow, this can exist even in small towns. In Korea, we established our first center just three years ago in Seoul. The UK had one in Bournemouth, a small town, over 10 years ago! For me, it was like this could be my inspiration. I went to the UN in Geneva to lobby the human rights committee and spoke to them about the

Korean government and its bad behavior toward LGBT society in Korea. […]. So, it's these things, connecting with other countries and sharing ideas.

By deploying a discourse that posits the West as progressive in terms of the advancement of LGBT+ and queer rights, Martin intimates the utility of a type of benchmarking for Korean queer activists; one that he sees has real political value in being able to mobilize political support and even resources. In fact, for his organization, the international connection was of great significance in being able to draw financial support from around the globe. The money that came from outside Korea was central to his organization being able to survive. His was a project that I had started donating to modestly when I lived in Seoul, and I continue to do so to this day.

> When this organization was established, we were funded from so many sources. We had some Korean donors; others are international, mostly US and UK donors. We made an account on global giving and most of the donors are from the UK and the US. Because the Korean American gay community helped us to financially set up originally – they held fundraising events and then sent us that money – and our biggest funding came from Google. The key money[10] [deposit] of our center, in grant form, was from Google. We got another part from the Beautiful Foundation, which is a benefactor for all minority groups in Korea, who funded us for three years. Every month we get individual donor support as well.

The diversity of participant backgrounds demonstrated that taking inspiration from movements and media of the West was not just a phenomenon that was restricted to activists. Jonathan, the next participant to be introduced, was an extroverted character. He was born, raised, and educated in Korea, and was pursuing university studies in the US. When we met, he was home for the summer, and I was introduced to him by one of my fellow New Zealanders. She had met him one night out clubbing in Hongdae. She said that he was openly gay, and through the course of our *talanoa*, Jonathan would relay to me how he felt it easier to make friends with foreigners in general, and gay foreigners in particular. Western cities like New York represented a type of aesthetic that he was attracted to. He was drawn into the New York style by television shows like *Gossip Girl*, a show that followed in the tradition of *Sex and the City*.

> *Gossip Girl was all about drama, and I felt so much guilty pleasure watching that show. And Sex and the City. I love New York, as it was set in New York City, my American dream comes from New York City. I just wanted to live surrounded by skyscrapers. They are fancy, elaborate, fashionable. Every region has its own style. New York has its own style, like a symbol of luxury.*

Jonathan's fascination with New York through television helped him to gain an appreciation of carefully manicured images of Western culture that he constructed discursively as more open, progressive, and elaborate than Korea. The effect of this type of discursive formation can also be seen in the responses that Sam, another Seoul participant, gave in relation to watching Western television programs; specifically, American shows. Sam came from a Catholic, modestly well-off family, and explained to me that his father was a strict authoritarian. His desire was to move out of Korea and live abroad, away from the restrictive confines of what a life in Korea would mean for him. He had just completed his military service when we completed his *talanoa*.

> **Patrick:** Do you think seeing gay characters in Western shows being normalized was helpful for you?
>
> **Sam:** I think so. You know I have never lived abroad. I was always curious about Western gay culture, how they live and get married. I learned from these programs like Modern Family.
>
> **Patrick:** What do you think you learned?
>
> **Sam:** Gay dating and gay marriage. Because in Korea, most gay guys just want to hook up, they don't want a relationship. Because in Korea it is illegal to get married. I don't think they are considering relationships seriously. I am tired of this. So, Western movies make me want to move out of Korea.

Sam desired to move to the fabled West to pursue a type of relationship that he saw as possible outside of Korea. The ability to view this as a viable path for him came through television. Gomillion and Giulano's (2011) empirical study on the influence of media role models on GLB youth showed that media platforms with GLB characters provided models that created sources of pride, inspiration, and comfort in their study set in Texas. Sam's responses seemed to mirror this finding and process. *Modern Family*, which he referenced, is a show that features a married gay couple that adopts children and raises them within an extended family network that normalizes their existence, a prospect that held great appeal to Sam.

Western television and musical icons were major factors in attracting participants to the liberating contours of Western discursive productions. For Soonchang, his time in Australia as an elementary and middle school student had helped to introduce him to Western celebrities. These Western experiences became central to his development and understanding of a gay subjectivity, and further sensitized him to the diversity of queer identities.

> I watched Will and Grace; it was funny. It was the fact that it was all about gay characters that interested me. Will and Jack, I liked Will better, Jack was hilarious, but back then he was too flamboyant. I was young at the time, so I thought about Jack's character in that way.

For Soonchang, the appeal of the show was mediated by the depiction of a gay masculinity as feminized. At first, he rejected Jack's character for being too flamboyant. The rejection of femininity has been identified by masculinities literature as common in the gay community. Battles and Hilton-Morrow (2002) analyzed *Will and Grace* using queer theory to articulate the liabilities of relying on the sitcom format to invite mainstream audiences to engage with gay characters. They argued that the show reinforced heterosexism by equating gayness with a lack of masculinity; a trait that Soonchang seemed to take objection to. He, however, learned to accept femininity as a trait that could be married with a gay masculinity when he went on to watch *Ru Paul's Drag Race*, a show that has been largely credited for helping to create greater awareness around the diversity of queer identities around the world (Edgar, 2011). Prior to this next excerpt, Soonchang had explained to me that he had dated primarily foreigners: White gay men who had exposed him to the show. As a result, he was able to develop a view of queer subjectivity that was less "dragphobic."

> I met a new guy in 2015 and he said you should watch it [Ru Paul's Drag Race]. We literally Netflixed and chilled all the seasons and I just loved it. Crack up and funny. But also, I don't know, when I was first dating my ex, I wasn't transphobic, maybe a little dragphobic? I didn't like the idea of gay people being portrayed feminine. That stereotype of how straight people think of gay people, when there are actually a lot of different types of gay people, you know what I mean? You can easily portray gay people like this. Even in Will and Grace, Jack was kind of like this. In movies they're always portrayed in fashion, flamboyant. I didn't like that idea at all, that was my justification of why I didn't like drag queens back then. But I've opened up since then, I went to gay clubs a lot and I'm at peace with it. Finally, I accepted, it's really fine to be whoever you are, a drag or whatever, that's why I got hooked into it.

Soonchang's responses were important in that he was familiar with colloquial terms that have become popular in English speaking countries such as, "Netflix and chill", which is a loaded term that has been taken up by millennials to mean several things, including code for (sometimes unplanned) sexual intimacy (Eble, 2017). However, he also demonstrated a process by which his exposure to Western television shows helped him to gain an awareness of gay stereotypes as discourses, and further that subsequent shows that he watched, also of US origin, helped him to critique the singularity of those discourses.

Lady Gaga – *Born This Way* and the power of pop music from the West

Soonchang's narrative is an exemplar of the power that Western media and cultural products carried in participant stories to circulate discourses and ideas around queer subjectivities and their liberation. The liberation narrative can also be demonstrated by the conversation we had around the types of music he listened to. Soonchang was not the only participant to reference Lady Gaga as someone he enjoyed listening to, specifically for the freedom it offered them as gay people. For example, Lady Gaga's song *Born This Way* was labeled by nearly all participants as a "gay anthem."

> When I was younger, I listened to Amy Winehouse, Coldplay, Britney Spears, and stuff, we're all gays. We all love Britney and of course Lady Gaga. Her music is big, Poker Face, Telephone, Born This Way – that was iconic. I liked it, I really liked the whole content of the song when I was 23 or 24, being born the way that you are. It was all about that thing.

Jeremy, who will feature later in this chapter, said that the lyrics, *"almost made me cry because it was about us, she was singing about us, making us free."* Paul, another participant, started singing it back to me during our *talanoa*; and Gene said that "Born This Way *really helped me to understand that it was OK to be who I was. You know, it's hard for me because I haven't really told anyone."* Jang

S. Mo and Lee Hoon (2014) examined how *Born This Way* was an example of popular music that could influence political attitudes. They concluded that it helped to prime genetic explanations of homosexuality as "natural," subsequently affecting the way citizens evaluated gay rights issues. For participants in my study, the sense of pride they felt helped them to feel a greater sense of comfort in coming to terms with their sexuality.

For Bob, the role of Western musicians was an important part of the journey toward understanding himself and his gay identity. As one of the older participants in the study, his narrative was important because his development of a gay identity came before the advent of the internet. Thus, I interpreted the temporality attached to that experience as heightening the importance of pop music artists, who in the 1990s tapped into globalizing forces around music distribution, circulating creative and ultimately liberating discourses around sexuality and sexual identity. I related to this experience, being a teenager in the same era, albeit in another part of the world, and living in a cultural context whose musical influences were often tied to popular US and UK artists. During the 90s, music was the primary way Bob learned about Western culture. Here, he emphasizes the role Western musicians played in helping him narrate his own story.

> Back then, I didn't know about the gay situation among musicians. But the more I listened to music and the more I got to know about particular musicians, I realized that they were related to gay society. Mariah Carey, Janet Jackson, and Madonna, they were huge fans of gay people, so they are somehow related to gay people. Music is very influential. Even the music that

people listen to in clubs was influenced by gay people. I am not a clubbing type person, I don't really know the club music scene well, but music is very related to gay culture, which tells a lot of my stories.

All that glitters: The allure of a Western coming-out story

The appeal of Western ideas was not limited to just television programs and musical icons. It also extended to the process of coming out itself. At a special event for the Solidarity for LGBT Human Rights in Korea (SLHRK) 20-year anniversary of its founding, I was introduced to my next participant: Chad. As is not uncommon when a foreigner arrives at an event hosted by Koreans, the person with the best English is usually sent to accompany the foreigner, and this task was assigned to him. He sat dutifully at my table for the remainder of the event and later agreed to meet me for a *talanoa* as part of my study. He had recently returned to Korea after completing his graduate studies in the US and had spent most of his life abroad in Southeast Asia before then. His narrative was important in that his exposure to the West was not indirect or mediated through a third party, but rather it came from direct exposure by going to university in America. It was there that Chad felt inspired to follow what he termed a particular "performative" coming-out narrative. Chad felt that the performative aspect of coming out – after much reflection on the disaster of his first coming-out to his parents – was, in his own words, "a very White narrative." He believed that there were specific differences between coming out in non-

White cultures that required more careful consideration. As such, he regretted the way that he did so the first time.

> Anyway, the whole American media spoiled me. I literally staged a coming-out for my fraternity; this was a thing you did, you see. I knew there was also a political element to it, I somehow needed to make a statement. It really is an American thing [performative coming-out], because as soon as it comes to a different country, the performative thing isn't the only way to live. There are huge cons to coming out in a performative way. But America sold it to me very well. It's a very White narrative. […] Here I was, a naïve 19-year-old who bought into that. I did it. I told my sister on a rainy July day. I know a guy who is around my sister's age and was active in the gay students' association. He came out to his mom and his mom was really supportive. He told me I should come out to my parents like him and that is when I can start the conversation. Yes, I listened to a friend from a single culture background. I would say now, think again when coming out. You need more planning.

Chad's "first" coming-out narrative (he would relay to me later that he had to come out again and again to his family), went badly. His mother took it the hardest and cried for many days. He regretted immensely listening to advice from someone who did not understand his own cultural context. His story, which is revisited later, demonstrates some of the risks associated with not having a culturally sensitive understanding of what challenges can emerge when applying queer logics of visibility born in the Western countries to your own. Chad's advice was to plan properly for a coming-out, and many of the participants of my study demonstrated that this was something that they were preparing themselves for in the future. The ability to re-negotiate their positions within the family as gay sons, as well as the ability to cultivate a self-reliance in the case of complete familial disintegration and abandonment, was something all participants held at the forefront of their minds.

Korean backwardness, Western benchmarking, and the winds of change

Aaron: Gay people have only just come out to the surface recently. Everybody is very new to this concept and at the same time does not know how to react to this. And even for gay people, we don't know how to explain and how to speak out. Which [makes it] very hard for us to request what we need and want. Gay society is quite young. We are too used to hiding in hidden places. We [are] still scared of coming out to other people. It is hard to talk about our natural daily gay lives at our work. I think we need to develop and learn more.

This excerpt from Aaron's *talanoa* demonstrates the type of discursive construct that was common among participant narratives: a construct that supposed a type of Korean gay community that needed to catch up with the West. For Aaron, Korean gay society was behind the West, and required gay men in Korea to gain courage from the path that had been trodden already by gay men in Western countries. This catching-up sentiment was one that Bob shared. Bob was an activist who worked with one of Korea's most well-known gay organizations[11] and was introduced earlier in the chapter. Bob also offered this in our *talanoa*:

> There are not enough resources to be able to educate people in Korea around the gay concept. I learned a lot about gay concepts through the media, music, and dramas. There was a magazine I remember called "buddy." I learned a lot about being gay through this magazine, I feel really sad because Korean society has a lack of resources to educate people about gay society.

Bob believed that many Koreans had the wrong understanding or conceptual grasp of what a gay sexual identity entailed. Often, he explained, gay men had been discursively constructed as carriers of HIV and AIDS, diseases that have also historically been linked to the foreign other in certain discourses circulated in South Korea (Wagner and Van Volkenburg, 2012). Indeed, when I attended the multiple pride events that are now being held all over South Korea, Christian fundamentalists often held up signs that urged the Korean state to protect their children from HIV and AIDS, which was incorrectly tied to homosexuality.

Other participants also emphasized how this association of AIDS with gayness was a practice that impacted their own lives growing up in Korea. Aaron talked about how he believed that this mindset began with older generations, and that an effort was also needed to educate the emerging generation about the specific differences between a gay identity and sexual health.

If we are waiting for the new generation, who will educate them? If the older generation people do, they will just hand out to the younger generation their biased ideas. Just like my friends who thought HIV equals gay. I think we need to make an effort to educate both.

As Woori Han (2018) explains, the cultivation of a queer developmental citizenship is an observable phenomenon in the discourses that circulate around queer festivals like the Seoul Queer Culture Festival. Han describes how participants in their study use a catching-up-to-the-West type of strategy to help mobilize support for the realization of gay rights in South Korea. Evidence of Han's assertions is clearly present in participants' narratives. However, participants storied these assertions as a type of temporality, positing that Korean society was living in a different time from the West when it came to gay rights. The division for them was generational, similar to what participants in Seattle had also storied regarding the fundamental bedrock feature of a Korean America version of Korean culture being embedded within an outdated image of Korean values and culture. Despite the temporal difference, the participants believed that Korea was catching up slowly. Soonchang explained it to me as a type of gradual but eventual change that would bring Korea more in line with what Martin called a global standard.

I think it's happening slowly, at a slow pace. Little by little, in that way the Korean gay community is being affected, I guess. This country will move forward on homosexuality. I see it everywhere. I've seen on YouTube, there are Korean gay tubers and trans YouTubers who host talk shows, using YouTube as a powerful platform these days. [...] If I have to compare gay guys in Korea in their 30s, 40s, 50s, there's a huge disparity because we are more comfortable. Comparatively we're more open, we're not discreet and that's proof of change.

The referencing of platforms like YouTube, made possible by technological innovation, must be seen as an important facilitating factor. When I spoke with Bob earlier, the only way he had been exposed to discourses around gay subjectivity and ideas he believed came from the West was through a music culture that came highly censored via the radio and magazines. Technological advancements present many more opportunities for transformation, especially for younger gay Koreans. This was a sentiment that was echoed by Martin himself, who was approaching his 40s and had witnessed the inception of the first prominent activist movements in Korea from the 1990s.

I see so many youths these days, and I can't compare them with my experience. They are more visible, and I'm sure they will be more visible as more and more time goes by.

The generational divide

Henry also storied the division between Korean social norms as backwardness, related to the temporal-specific Korean context. Namely, his explanation focused on generational temporalities and a type of conservative residue that can be traced to this generational difference. According to him, those who were driving both mainstream essentialist discourses around Korean gay men, and also the resistance to their integration in Korea, found their reference points in the era of the Park Chunghee dictatorship:

> Back in the 1970s era of dictatorship, they did not want diversity. They wanted to easily control people. Even at that time, there were a lot of protests against the dictatorship. But those people are still conservative when it comes to LGBT issues. What they have in mind is anti-dictatorship politics, but the scope of their minds has not developed and expanded to other sectors. So, it is very disappointing, the current President [Moon Jae-in] was a protestor back then, but his mentality still remains in that era.

Henry's referencing of this temporality in the differences in people's understanding of reform and protest, by not expanding and adapting to incorporate contemporary forms of diversifying sexual identity in their understanding created a type of generational dichotomy between his generation and the protestors and activists of the past. In doing so, he was inevitably couching his take on the Korean perspective as one that paired Korean conservatives with a backwardness on sexual diversity that was a result of generational difference and the passage of time. But this temporality had found itself extended into contemporary times and was exacerbated by the continued privilege of a heteronormative frame among Korean masculinities.

> I have an impression of the difference between Westerners and Koreans. I came out to most of my foreign friends and female friends. Korean men are reluctant to accept LGBT rights. This is what I discovered.

A few weeks ago, I came out to my French friend, and
he was very supportive because he has a few lesbian
friends. I also think Korean women are more accepting
than Korean men as this has to do with gender roles.
As Confucianism is still pervasive in Korea, it says men
should act in a "manly" way, which I relate to mandatory
military service. Still, in Korea [in the military], there is a
ridiculous and outdated rule that says that those who
commit anal sex will go to prison for two years. Sexual
intercourse between a man and female is OK, but
between a man and man is considered a crime. That is
not acceptable in my opinion.

In recounting the obvious injustices and uneven application of
anti-sodomy laws in the military, Henry inevitably draws on a
discursive frame that posits the Korean position as one that is
outdated, oppressive, and backward. In doing so, he juxtaposes,
on top of his statement, the progressiveness of the West against
the barbarism of the Korean state's biopolitical disciplining of
the homosexual body. This is a generative tactic, which can
help to constitute the relative victimhood of marginalized
sexual identities in South Korea and represents a productive
modality of Western discourses on sexual politics. The tactic was
deployed by participants in our *talanoa* to urge political action
and change in the local, Korean context, represented by the state
and its institutions. The tactic, however, casts Korea as steeped
in backwardness; a position that must be articulated against a
progressive standard they saw in the West.

For Silas, another Seoul participant, the backwardness of Korean
social norms around sexuality and non-heterosexual relationships
can be evidenced through the way the Korean media censored

stories that came from the US. Specifically, Silas purported that stories which reported on progress made in Western societies around LGBT rights were being discursively "othered" by Korea's media. Having recently returned to Seoul from Shanghai, Silas was a well-known drag artist "on the scene," and had been featured in a few newspaper articles in both Korea and abroad. Silas became a key participant throughout the year, helping to introduce me to many people within Seoul's rapidly burgeoning drag scene. The frustrations that Silas felt were related to how the Korean media presented or stayed silent on major events that affected the gay community abroad, like the Pulse night club shooting in Florida.

> I'm trying to stay away from the Korean media because they make me so angry. I saw how they reacted in Korea [when the Pulse night club shooting happened] and they made it seem like an ordinary night club shooting. Not mentioning that it was a hate crime against the LGBT community. It wasn't until there was some backlash from the community here that they finally reported it as a gay club that was targeted. Seeing behavior like that makes me realize that Korea is still very conservative.

Again, the issue for Silas was the backwardness of the normative practices of the Korean media. Putting aside the issue of how the media can drive the production of mainstream discourses in general, the discursive practice of pitching Korea as backward was something that continued through the narratives of all participants. Martin was able to add a bit more depth and nuance to the practice by referencing a historical frame in describing why he believed Western normative structures carried a productive element that related to benchmarking.

> In my own opinion, Korean people don't think that Western culture is bad; they see it is OK, or better than our own Korean culture. They "other" some things as "Western culture" but they don't think it's bad. Inside them, Korean people don't want to go back to Korean traditional culture. People don't think that Western people are bad.

For Martin, the relationship between Korea and the West was one in which, for many Koreans, there was an admiration for what the West had achieved, complicating our readings of the impacts of American hegemony. While the rapidly spreading liberating contours of Western normative constructs around divergent sexuality can be critiqued for its neocolonial slippages through the lens of homonationalism, it appears that many participants have a suspicion that Western approaches to sexual identity integration are just better than Korea's backward and conservative reality. This is not to say that participants accepted Western superiority blindly; in fact, they resisted other areas of Western influence, particularly when it came to experiences of racism and microaggressions, which will be developed further in subsequent chapters of this book.

What participant narratives offer here is a more complex rendering of the relationship between the West and South Korea's queer community. Power imbalances in the way forms of queer representation remain nestled within Euro-American symbols and labels of gender and sex non-normativities and the associated politics. These norms and agitations for political change still represented a benchmark that participants believed gave them political utility in pursuing their own desires to reform the units of power that governed Korean gay bodies and movements within their own local context.

Discussion questions

Is there a global standard around what queer or gay identities are meant to embody?

What insights does this chapter offer us in understanding the multifaceted realities tied to the concept of homonationalism?

In what ways do you think our understandings of queer identities are tied to a global norm and practice that circulates from the great queer metropoles of North America (New York, Chicago, Toronto, Los Angeles, San Fransisco), Europe (London, Berlin, Amsterdam) and the Global North (Sydney)?

What liabilities lie in relying on a catching-up-to-the-West type of strategy or a homonationalist politic to develop queer acceptance in non-Western contexts?

What impact do you think expanding technologies will have on the development of queer and gay identities across the world?

Notes

9. Some participants in Seoul intimated that there was a discursive code around knowing how to read which spaces in the popular Jongno district were gay establishments. There was a specific way signage was written that allowed gay men to know that these were safe spaces for them to congregate.

10. In South Korea, "key money" is a large deposit amount given to landlords, which they in turn invest, usually in term-deposits that yields them large interest. In return, renters usually pay a smaller monthly amount of rent. In Seoul, key

money usually starts around 5 million won, or equivalent to $5,000 in local money. For a center or large office space, the amount can be closer to 50 million won, or $50,000 in local currency. Sometimes landlords will only require a key money deposit and no rent is paid for a fixed term. In that case, the key money can reach over 100 million won, or $100,000 in local currency.

11. The name of the organization has been redacted for confidentiality.

5
Negotiating queer/ gay futurity in Seoul

Chaggi Kwalli and the cultivation of the self-reliant queer self

When I first met Aaron, he had just exited a long-term relationship with an American and was volunteering at an NGO dedicated to promoting the prevention of AIDS and HIV in South Korea. He was also working with a local government organization, and we crossed paths in the Seoul queer scene just as I was preparing to move to Seattle to begin my doctoral studies. We kept in touch while I was in the US, and he was one of the first people I contacted, when I arrived back in Seoul, about possible participation in the study. I was particularly interested in talking with him upon my return as he was the only Korean gay man (up until that point) I had met on the scene who had undergone a complete coming-out to his parents.

> I've come out to everyone, but only my immediate family. That's my dad, my mom, and sister, but not my extended family. It was my dad that asked me not to tell them. I guess

it was because of the humiliation or some kind of stress it might be for him from me going against the norm. [...] He did want to know why it took me so long to come out, because I knew I was gay when I was 15, so it took me about 10 years to come out. I said to him when I came out that I had waited to tell them because I was not independent, I was not ready financially, and had to rely on my parents. They could have used their power to rule over me and they could try to change me. I was worried about that and I didn't really know who I was either at the time. I decided that I needed time to define who I was and waited for the perfect timing before I came out.

In this first excerpt from our *talanoa*, Aaron detailed threads that were to become a familiar theme across participants I worked with in Seoul. Aaron's decision to also wait until he was financially independent – when read in line with the concept of *Chaggi Kwalli*, or *self-reliance*, as defined by Nancy Abelmann and colleagues (2013) – make contextual sense. This individual subjectivity (Campbell, 2016), driven by the pressures and excesses of a hyper capitalist Korean society, has resulted in shifts in Korean relationalities away from group and family and toward the individual, primed to meet the cosmopolitan realities of the contemporary job market. This idea, however, has not been explored much in the context of Korean gay men's coming-out narratives. The increased need for self-reliance within South Korean society as a whole has been focused on by queer Korean scholars such as John Song Pae Cho (2020), who uses the lens of neoliberal subjectivities to help understand how shifts in socio-economic-political conditions have reshaped queer life and subjectivities in South Korea.

Self-reliance, or the ability to support oneself financially, as a major factor impacting a coming-out narrative was a common theme for many participants, including Jonathan, whose story enters our discussion here. Jonathan was from a middle-to-upper-class family (self-identified). The issue of self-reliance was one that he was very concerned about. Jonathan spoke about the great relationship he had with his family, including a gentle father who had taught him to be good to others and a caring mother who he was extremely close to. When it came to the issue of coming out, he most feared the effect on his parents as opposed to the effect it would have on him. In order to protect his parents, as well as himself, he thought the best thing he could do was prepare to be independent.

Patrick:	You haven't come out to your parents yet, do you have a desire to?
Jonathan:	Yes, I want to come out to my sister first, but the only reason why I don't want to come out is because they will worry about me. They will worry about my future life and, still, they worry about my current life. They are always concerned about me. By the time I have full independence, have my own house, own job, then I am going to come out to them.
Patrick:	So, your hesitation is due to your worry about how it would affect your parents?
Jonathan:	Yes
Patrick:	Do you think they would disown you?
Jonathan:	I am preparing for that as well, in a way; that's why I want to come out to my family once I am

independent. I'm such a bad son for saying this, but if they don't accept who I am, I will live my own life and they will live their own and we don't have to talk anymore [laughter].

Despite Jonathan mentioning that his cultivation of an independent self is to ensure survival of his future gay self, the connection to his family is undeniable. His decision about coming out is still constructed around maintaining his family's wellbeing, seeking to protect them any way he can. The fact that he reprimands himself for mentioning the possibility of living a separate life from his parents is significant. His type of imagined futurity clearly juxtaposes the group/familial responsibility he feels with being prepared to disavow the support structure he found in his family in the event of their refusal to accept his decision to claim a gay identity publicly. In considering this juxtaposition, Jonathan enacts a queer worldmaking practice which seeks to imagine a future in which a queer subject is able to thrive beyond the confines of heteronormative structures, time, and space.

Strategizing, coming out in Seoul, and renegotiating familial roles and spaces

Jonathan was not the only participant to demonstrate this practice of queer worldmaking tied to an imagined future beyond a heteronormative South Korean society and in relation to a coming-out narrative. These complex practices were closely referential with respect to their families. This imagined queer futurity and worldmaking contrasted strongly with how they spoke of Korean society as being backward and conservative. Korean families, to participants, produce multiple discourses of both inclusion and exclusion, which are related to different forms of Korean familism (familial archetypes) and divergences in education and income background. Take, for example, Henry's story of coming out. Henry is from a middle-to-upper-class family and enjoys quite a high position in the Korean public service. He travels a lot for work and has plans to migrate abroad. When his family found out he was gay, rather than shun him, they tried to understand him, and even participated in meetings for the parents of LGBT children.

> It was two years ago, back in 2015. At that time, I used to live alone in Seoul. My mother came to see me sometimes. And once I was not home but my mother came over and found some books that I got from the gay festival in Seoul. It was a book about homosexuality. So, she just took in the fact that I am gay. My father was somewhat calm because he knew I used to hang out with only girls and had a lot of gut feelings while I grew up. So later they had no choice but to accept it. They participated twice in the LGBT parents meeting. They try to figure out what is good for me. I wanted to immigrate to other countries. Before I came out, my parents didn't want me to go abroad. But now that they know I am gay, they are trying to understand. They try to respect my decision.

When Henry and I spoke after the recorded *talanoa*, he relayed to me that his parents felt it was probably best that he did move abroad for his own sake. They feared for the difficult life he would have to endure living in South Korean society as a gay man. This response is interesting from a variety of standpoints. It appears that, initially, Henry's desire to move abroad was a decision he made on his own without explicit parental agreement. Activating a queer mobility so he could build a queer futurity in another place whilst imagining it in the here and now in South Korea. However, his parents eventually came to support his decision as they came to understand the dangers for their son. The strategic response from his parents in this case I relate to affectionate familism. Despite Henry transgressing a heteronormative construct by coming out as gay, he is still the child of a Korean family that has been constructed as the central site of social welfare and support. His parents have taken this responsibility seriously in recognizing the difficulties he would face living a life in South Korea. In doing so, they are accepting their role in keeping their family safe and intact.

Another participant who had come out and maintained a positive relationship with his family was Jeremy. I met Jeremy by chance at the same SLHRK event in Seoul where I encountered Chad. Jeremy had been in a relationship with his boyfriend for five years prior to coming out and decided to come out to his mother while watching television. On that fateful day, Hong Seok-chon, the first openly gay Korean celebrity, had appeared on television. Upon seeing him, his mother blurted out that she thought he had a "disorder," or 문란 inCharacter not converting correctly. Korean. Jeremy, enraged, decided that he would reveal his sexuality to her at 16 years old.

> She cried. She couldn't imagine that she had a gay son, me, and that she had to endure such a life, a difficult life. She wanted to know why I didn't tell her earlier. She

began to tell the rest of my family and now everyone is
OK with me being gay.

Although at first things were difficult for Jeremy's parents to
accept, they came to accept his sexuality after a period of familial
discussion and of constant renegotiation of expectations and
roles for him within the family. What is important about Jeremy's
narrative is that he was from a low-income family and his parents
came to accept his gay identity once he was able to demonstrate
his own independence. Jeremy had once wanted to become
a priest, having been raised Catholic. But after being told that
he was a "sinner" by the Church, he abandoned that dream to
go into social work, where he now advocates for the rights of
disabled communities and is a labor rights activist. He said he
felt compelled to do social work and activism after experiencing
much discrimination as a teenager, having come out so early.
What Jeremy's narrative suggests is that affectionate familism as
a lens clarified how he and his family renegotiated his position
within the family. Once he was able to prove his ability to support
himself, the concerns from his parents about his sexuality began
to wane.

Navigating familial pressure and the harsh realities of militarism

Particular forms of familism articulated themselves in other,
less comfortable, ways, through the coming-out process for
other participants. Vincent's story of coming out was one of
forced trauma; a type of trauma that was only complicated
and muddled by the different archetypes of Korean familism.
When I met him, Vincent was working for one of my friends at

a bar in Seoul's foreigner district, having completed his military service. Although the details were a little hazy, it appeared that attempts had been made to make an example of him for being a whistleblower against sexual abuse in the Korean military.

> I was friendly with some of the superior officers, and they used to make me lick the inside of their mouths. […] One day they wanted us to give feedback and most people wrote silly stuff like: "I am doing good," "I am satisfied," but I really wanted to change this one thing. But the way feedback was given was done openly. You had to put up your hand. But this was stupid because people were gathered very close to each other. So, when I raised my hand the person next to me knew. One day, the sexual abusers – the soldiers – went to jail, and they thought the gay soldiers like me were troublesome, so they sent us to the mental hospital. They tried to make us have a problem and tried to kick us out. They required me to tell one of my parents in the process. So I talked to my sister. I said I liked guys, and she said "I knew it;" she told me to come out to my mom. […] I told my mom, and she was very shocked. She suggested that I was confused because I am very artistic and sensitive. My mum knows but she pretends she doesn't know.

The complications of Vincent's story brought together many discourses that circulate around gay men in South Korea, not the least being the oppressive biopolitical frame that functions as a type of Foucauldian governmentality (Foucault et al., 1991) in the Korean military. The military acts as an agent of state power that works insidiously to control and regulate the bodies of gay men in South Korea. The biopolitical strategy of the Korean state is well documented and was famously traced by Seungsook Moon's (2005) exemplary book *Militarized Modernity and Gendered Citizenship in South Korea*. Vincent's narrative illuminated the still considerable biopolitical powers of the Korean state in contemporary times. This was evidenced by the way that he was subject to dubious charges of mental illness, designed to set him up as a deviant body requiring regulation and, as a result, a dishonorable discharge from the military. The fact that Vincent was required to tell one of his parents that he was gay was another example of this type of governmentality and the state intrusion into the affairs of the South Korean family that exists today. Vincent's mother's response was not pleasant, and he had been subjected to continual conversion practices at the time we held our *talanoa*.

For Anton, the issue of familial tension was one that also loomed large when his sexual identity was discovered by his parents. When I met Anton, he was sitting at a table on his own at the end of a Church service where I had also met Martin earlier. I approached him after Martin asked if he would be interested in speaking to me about my research. Anton decided to meet me a week later in a café near his home in one of Seoul's wealthier neighborhoods. Our *talanoa* ended up lasting for nearly two hours as he relayed to me some of his own perspectives about gay life in Korea. He was the only child of a "Seoulite couple," spent years studying abroad, and was rather savvy about some of the latest Western discourses of queer theory and queer social movements. Anton explained that his own coming-out story was a particularly distressing experience for him, in which his parents brought into sharp relief the importance of the divide between the family and an unprogressive Korean society constructed by Anton as an existential threat to any family that harbored a gay son.

> When I was 16, I was going through puberty and of course I started looking at pornographic materials while I was learning about sexual things. I watched gay porn on my personal computer at home and my parents discovered it when I was at home. […] My parents' reaction was very negative. My mother hated it, but my father said that there are many different types of people in this world. But our society is not progressive. Korea is not ready to accept these people. […] Do not choose the hard way

For Anton's father, the issue was not whether he should accept or reject his son, it was whether his son would be able to survive in Korean society. For Anton– and for all participants, in fact – parents, family, and their preservation were of utmost concern. Although the idea of staunch heterosexism within Korean society and familial structures has been well-telegraphed, as Wang and colleagues (2009) detail in the Taiwanese Confucian context, roles as sons in the Korean family become negotiated once a coming-out takes place. Coleman and Chou (2000), when speaking of the term *Tongzhi* or comrade as a marker for queer identities in Chinese societies, reference the importance of familial kinship systems rather than sexuality as the taken basis of an individual's identity. Jackson and colleagues (2013) also argue that homosexuality, as a constructed existential threat in East Asian societies, is better understood through the lens of the challenge it presents to patriarchal normative structures of the family as opposed to a heterosexist one.

In line with this reasoning, Anton's response and choice of words demonstrated the way in which "gay" was being discursively constructed by participants and other members of their family as an "other," much like the way Seo Dongjin (2001) had described. Gay people were referred to as "these people" as if they sat outside the sphere of Korean society. The idea of gay, discursively constructed by participants and those around them, was not only an "other," it was also Western; an idea that sat in direct opposition to the hegemonic heteronormative ideals that pervade South Korea's public sphere.

The role of Christianity

Patrick: How do you resolve being a Christian and being gay in Korea? As we know, the Christian community is aggressive in stopping the advancement of LGBT minorities.

Anton: Frankly speaking, I haven't really resolved the problem. It's still complicated in my mind. How to reconcile that relationship; I've thought about it very much and still no conclusion.

The role of Christian fundamentalists in blocking progress in South Korea is well noted in popular and academic literature. Despite a strong understanding of the role that Christianity has played in preventing recent progress on queer liberation, Anton still attended Church and openly identified as a Christian. In this way, Anton represented many participants in both Seoul and Seattle, who were also strong Christians. Marrying the two positions was no easy task, and was one whose complexity was understood in its historical context by many participants.

> I think Christianity in modern Korea has been a modernizing force because when the Protestant Church was first introduced to Korea, many missionaries founded schools, by American missionaries or so. The Catholic church even before that. When Koreans first got to learn Catholic things, it was kind of an enlightenment for the Joseon dynasty. It had some kind of egalitarian doctrine. [...] Nowadays, the Christians are the main enemy to progress in contemporary Korea.

Anton's response mirrors what has been written about the historical genealogy of the Korean Christian Church. Clark (1986) wrote a comprehensive historiography on the history of the Korean Christian Church in English that supports Anton's statements. Further to this, according to Cho Min-Ah (2011), Christian conservatives saw their political influence wane at the successful ushering in of democracy in Korea at the end of the 1980s. Cho argues that Christian conservatives once found their power in the anti-communist discourse perpetuated by the authoritarian state. Once the authoritarian state disappeared, so did their opportunity for defining the "other" and essentializing it as an enemy of the state.

Anton was not the only participant to grapple with the issue of religion when coming out. Silas' narrative brought forth the intertwined nature of Christianity with the Korean diaspora in the US. Having spent most of his formative years in the US, Silas indicated that his family had fallen into a Christian Korean American community in California. Not unlike participants I encountered in Seattle, it was the Church network that had helped set his family up in California and that supported them as they transitioned across the Pacific.

> My entire family are Jehovah's Witnesses. Right when we moved to America, my mom got help from other Witnesses. They were a Korean congregation, they helped us in going to school and moving in. […] The thing with Jehovah's Witnesses is that I was born into it. I didn't have a say whether I liked my religion or not. I was forced to attend these meetings. But as I started to figure out what I was, my mentality began to crash. I told my mom in high school [in the US] and she broke down and said: no. She told me that I am going through a phase. So, I kept it hidden. Then I went onto college, and I became more forward. I told her "Hey I'm gay, I have a boyfriend." She stopped talking to me, stopped my allowance, and didn't even support my tuition for college. It was a very rough year for me. […] After that, I didn't talk to my mom for three months, I had to juggle different jobs and stuff. Eventually she realized she loves me more than religion.

The role of religion had a profound impact on Silas' positionality within the family, like many of the Seattle participants had intimated and reported in previous chapters. In building their social support networks through the Church, the participants' familial structure was affected by Christian normative constructs, so much so that Silas was nearly disowned when he decided to come out. Later, his mother came around, and Silas was now studying again. What marks Silas' narrative out as separate from other participants in Seoul is that he spent most of his formative years in the US, meaning he was directly exposed to Western constructs of sexual visibility, including what can be considered the linear coming-out process. This represented a reversal of transnational flows, suggesting that the impact of the Korean American Christian Church was not geographically locked, but was in fact a two-way movement of ideas and practices.

The connection between Christianity and Western normative constructs in this context is a multilayered one. In Korea, both Christianity and Western normative constructs came from outside, centered in Euro-American locations. Christianity was once an emancipatory force on the peninsula but is now seen as an impediment to social progress by participants. Sexual identity politics or sexual exceptionalism embodied in the discourses that seek the liberation of queer, namely gay, subjects share the same geographic, historical, and genealogical roots as Christianity: the West.

Temporal and teleological obfuscation helped to elide the connectedness both these discourses, Christianity and modernity, share in a history that ties power to ideas that come from outside Korean society and culture. In other words, although they seemingly represent different positions regarding sexuality, their entry was premised on a power-configuration that places them as superior, progressive, and modern, from places that we from the Global South see as colonial metropoles to aggressively push against in the quest to Indigenize and decolonize. As such, the multiple discourses being produced in South Korea's gay and queer communities, when read in relation to the social and political shifts that have impacted the Korean family and Korean familism archetypes, suggest that coming out in Korea is much more complex than simply a movement toward modernity; especially when ideas of modernity regarding globalizing sexual and gender liberation are tied up within geopolitical scripts of homonationalist global politics.

Discussion questions

Considering the intense complexities of the Korean family detailed here and throughout this book, what does it mean to negotiate a queer futurity?

What similarities/differences do you see between the participants in Seoul and the participants in Seattle, regarding the complications of coming out?

What do you see as the difference between negotiating futurities within a framework of *Chaggi Kwalli* versus the strategizing required to develop a narrative of convenience documented in Seattle?

How do the reflections offered in this chapter nuance our understanding of the role of Christianity in restricting queer futurities in the Korean context?

How does this chapter complicate our readings of the role of foreigners and foreign constructs in the context of queer realities in Korea?

6

Seattle so gay white: Unpacking the experiences of racism among Korean gay men

Cain: What's that saying? Seattle's so gay, but what it really is, is Seattle's so gay White"

White gay men are often centered as the symbol of the gay community. This type of privilege creates a hierarchy of desire that places them at the apex of racial hierarchies in many settler societies (Bérubé, 2001; Teunis, 2007). Seattle is routinely named one of the most gay-friendly cities in the US. From its vibrant queer district in Capitol Hill, to its gay mayor and liberal politics, the Emerald City shines with rainbows whilst being surrounded by fields of conservative red across Washington State. However, this narrative and experience is complicated by the ever-burgeoning scholarship critiquing the racism that exists in gay communities in the US and other anglosphere countries (Giwa, 2022; Han, 2007n) This suggests that for Queer People of Color (QPoC), queer liberational politics comes with many racialized caveats, complicated by experiences of racism tied to exclusion, objectification, and racialized tropes that proliferate not only in the experiences of participants shared in this chapter, but also in the wider literature around gay racism in America (Han and Choi, 2018; Stacey and Forbes, 2022).

Gay racism in America and the Asian American community

Despite the growing visibility of queer communities of color, the mainstream gay community and its political aspirations remain White in its orientation.

— Teunis (2007, p. 263)

For Teunis (2007), sexual objectification is a product of racism in the gay community that simultaneously allows for the production and the positioning of the White gay categorization as the idealized center. This occurs because ideologies of inclusivity and non-discrimination blind White gay men to the harmful effects of sexual objectification. Moreover, this sexual objectification forces men of color to play specific roles in sexual encounters that are not necessarily of their own choosing. Teunis' research found that White men were shown to be using racialized tropes to create their own sense of sexual freedom at the expense of the agency of Black men. Black men in their study storied ways in which White men expected them to take hypermasculine, top (insertive) roles in the bedroom; roles that were linked to racialized stereotypes, even against their own sexual preferences. At the same time, within community activism, Black organizers were only seen as capable of taking leadership roles that served minority gay populations specifically. As such, they were denied leadership roles that would allow them to drive more intersectionality informed social justice work in mainstream gay spaces.

In the Asian American context, studies orbiting around race highlight the fraught nature of the specific experience of Asian American gay men. For instance, Chong-suk Han (2008a) used critical race theory in their provocatively titled article "No Fats, Femmes or Asians" by adding that Asian American gay men were also subjected to racialization from within a gay community that set the White gay man as the reference point. Han and other scholars in Asian American studies (Chan, 1992; Chung and Katayama, 1998; Chung and Szymanski, 2006; Cochran et al., 2007; Harris, Battle, and Pastrana, 2017; Leong, 1996; Narui, 2011; Tsunokai, McGrath, and Kavanagh, 2014) have identified common stock narratives that deeply affect the Asian American gay male experience. These stock or standardized narratives advance essentialist notions of identity representation that subject Asian American gay men to (1) a model minority myth, (2) demasculinization through their constitution, seen as being effeminate and having small penises, (3) the notion that they are ripe for White consumption, and (4) the notion that they are trapped within an ultra-conservative cultural community deeply embedded within religious structures (Eguchi, 2011; Fung, 2005; Han, 2008a, 2008b; Ocampo and Soodjinda, 2016; Phua, 2007) (see Han, 2008a and b; Fung, 1996; Eguchi, 2010; Phua, 2007; Ocampo and Soodjina, 2016 and others).

In attempting to talk back to and challenge these dominant narratives that center White ways of knowing, Chong-suk Han (2008a) advocates for both the theoretical use and methodological approach of critical race theory, which advocates for an epistemology that reformulates both our understanding and the power relationships that are formed through racialization (Delgado and Stefancic, 2017). Critical race theorists and indigenous scholars advocate for the use of counter-narratives (telling a different, compelling story) to reclaim dehumanizing stock narratives (essentialist tropes), centering on the experiences of Black Indigenous people and People of Color (BIPOC), to privilege marginalized voices and elevate BIPOC interpretations of events and stories of events. Story-telling is a powerful tool that finds much congruence with Pacific, Samoan, and Indigenous epistemologies, and which highlights the generative potential of stories as a site of knowledge generation (Archibald et al., 2019). This chapter and the one that follows sit in conversation with these urgencies and insights.

Becoming the racialized other in Seattle

Cain: I think that these spaces of queer PoC that are exclusive are so important; that they only have the voices of these folks that belong to this community. […] Primarily, in my experience, I've dated mostly White, cis-bodied, gay LGBT males. […] In terms of the PoC community, it's been a lot harder to approach the cis White gay men that I've dated/interacted with [about this]. I've heard some really unpleasant things regarding race. There's racism in the gay community here. If you look on Grindr or OkCupid, all this research on the hierarchy of racial preference, it's really disgusting. I've also tried to steer away from dating White men, but that's something that's proving really difficult. That's also something I'm trying to unpack.

As an organizer in Seattle, Cain had been forced to grapple with the issue of race in queer spaces. Cain was not alone in identifying racism in the US gay community as part of their experience. Throughout this chapter, participants will share their general experience of racism in the city, adding to the numbers of challenges they negotiated in their lives. Their assertion was that, despite the openness of Seattle to queerness, there was still a need for spaces where queer BIPOC can congregate and live in their own truths. These experiences are often tied to practices of marginality that intersect where their race and queerness meet.

The works of Lisa Duggan and Jasbir Puar are both useful here. As Lisa Duggan (2002) details in her theory of the new homonormativity, gay men have been assimilated through a variety of neoliberal practices that draw them into commitments to reproduce normative structures tied to the privilege of men, despite being gay. Puar's (2013) extension of the new homonormativity into homonationalism demonstrates how cis gay men are drawn into the reproduction of the settler state as a salvageable queer subject capable of defending the interests of American imperialism. This role, according to Puar, is also one that is racialized; the question of how well you treat your homosexuals becomes the barometer for state legitimacy, much in the way liberal politics in the 1980s and early 1990s focused on the question of women.

What Cain's excerpt also demonstrates is that despite their own awareness of being a racialized subject, constituted as a lesser other through racialized discourses, they still felt attracted to dating White men. Again, this practice can be understood through the work of race scholars. One feature of racialization is that it not only creates racialized others, but it also distributes desire along hierarchies of power. In other words, the dominant racial group compels subjugated groups to continue to desire bodies that embody the racialized ideal that's tied to standards that define and position Whiteness as most desirable, through the allure of power. This ideal is especially evident in the US context.[12]

Moreover, Cain's experiences with being racialized as other was not limited to their interactions with cisgender White men that they were encountering. Toward the end of Chapter 2, when Cain was first introduced in this study, they talked about their experiences of going through therapy whilst dealing with their emerging gay identity. I present that particular passage here again now for emphasis:

> I've been trying to see therapists lately, and it's with this White lady at the moment, and after I've been telling her about what I'm going through, her response was simple: "Why don't you move out?" I wanted to scream at her, "Lady, I'm Korean. It's not that easy!"

I point to this interaction and our subsequent discussion as an introductory indicator to the ordinary ways in which racialization affected the daily lives of Seattle participants. Critical race theory argues that racism is not aberrational, but rather is ordinary and can be seen in the way everyday interactions are structured. I add that it can also appear well meaning and unintentional. By assuming that Cain would be able to "just move out," the therapist had unintentionally re-inscribed the ascendancy of her worldview above Cain's. In doing so, she was not only being culturally insensitive, but she also constituted them as a racial other: a position that Cain was forced to claim in this interaction by pointing out the difference in their worldview to validate their experience.

I argue that it is in these moments that racialization is at its most dangerous. The invisibility of worldviews that inform the way non-White people navigate their realities sets up a situation where the care they need is neglected and can further perpetuate harm. This harm that is a result of a single worldview – the default, dominant one – being able to speak above and for queer PoC, but that harm that can go completely unnoticed if the way healthcare is structured and determined by racial hierarchies is not also taken into consideration.

A racialized life in Seattle

We face challenges not as much as gay parents. My husband is Caucasian; I am a minority, LGBT person; kind of a triple negative. Racial profiling is a big thing, in terms of sexuality. We live in a place where everyone is tolerant; before we even get to the sexuality issue, there's the racial issue to deal with. My husband doesn't experience it like I do but he understands that there is racial prejudice. For instance, two years ago, when we went to Spokane, we stayed downtown. He and my redhead child ran into Starbucks. There was a Caucasian homeless woman asking him for money. My daughter was like, "Daddy, I want to give the woman money," and the lady was so responsive with her, saying, "Oh, poor

> baby," but then me, my Chinese kid, and my biracial
> child, three of us holding hands who were following
> behind, approached her. The same woman spat at us
> as we were going in, saying, "I don't want your money."

This excerpt from Barnabas' *talanoa* carries in it many coded ways of marking social hierarchy. For one thing, Barnabas and his husband are both aware of how they experience and perceive issues of race from different positions. And the tacit acknowledgement from Barnabas' husband also demonstrates how he understands the way he is implicated in the process. As Barnabas can story his own marginalization as the other, he uses his husband's status as a Caucasian man as a reference point in which he understands his racial marginalization. Further to this, the difference in treatment, where he is spat at by a homeless woman whilst his husband and his redhead are welcomed as generous, and caring is clearly evidence of hierarchical constructs of race and racism.

Another incident that showed how racialization coded him as an outsider took place among what Barnabas called "soccer moms" at the school his children attended. There were women whom, he explained, "don't know what to do with me!" As a gay father, he found that women in the PTA at his local school loved him and his husband, but issues of race and racialization presented as an area of low literacy for many he associated with.

> In this city, it is wonderful, but then ignorance is more
> a problem than blatant prejudice. For example, I like to
> entertain people. Once I said I'll make sushi and kids
> can learn how to make sushi with me (a week before
> Christmas. Everyone's gathering except for one mother.

Half an hour later, she walks in out of breath. "Sorry Barnabas, we were at Nordstrom to visit Santa" where most of us go every Christmas season. She goes: "Well, there was an Asian Santa. We didn't want the Asian Santa. So, we waited and waited till the White Santa came." I don't think she understood that I'm Asian, I don't think she meant to say that. She probably thought that we are just one of them. I don't think she meant it; she thinks we were White. When you think of ideology of race and racism, it's more like, once you get to know them, those categories start to dissipate, you just become one of them. For me, I live with it. She doesn't have to live with it.

Critical race theory is suspicious of liberalism and its scripts of equality, where treating everyone the same or providing procedural rights, as an example, cannot effectively deal with the racialized disparity experienced as outcomes for diverse racial and ethnic groups (Pyle, 1998). For Barnabas, his connection to his fellow parents in the PTA is clearly derived on the basis of his status as a parent. And the fact that these women welcomed him and his husband as gay dads speaks to a type of equality afforded to gay couples in Seattle. However, this incident highlights the insidious and slippery nature of racialization and racism at the intersections, where being "accepted" by a certain community, despite one's queerness, does not mean one's race is ever *really* "forgiven" in that context. In fact, what Barnabas is perceptive of in this excerpt is how familiarity, as a result of being embraced as queer or gay, is exactly **the** mechanism that allows race and racism to rise to the surface and become known. In accepting and creating a queer connection with Barnabas, the woman saw no real issue with dismissing the Asian Santa to a Korean man in a Korean man's house. Like Barnabas said, she doesn't have to live with it, but he does.

Critical race theory scholars argue that one feature of racism is its gaslighting of its victims (Roberts and Andrews, 2013). Gaslighting is a type of emotional abuse where the abuser deflects responsibility by provoking the receiver, through manipulation, to believe that the harm or impact is just an effect of their own imagination or mental instability (Wozolek, 2018). In this situation, Barnabas apologized on behalf of his racializer in our *talanoa*. Although not exactly racial gaslighting, this lens is helpful in situating and understanding what Barnabas recalled as a form of colorblind racism (Bonilla-Silva, 2018). This form of racism is where the racializer says they do not see color; however, by treating Barnabas as just another White person due to what she probably saw as an intrigue between friends and co-conspirators, her forgetful moment of his race inadvertently denies him full agency at the utterance of a single, careless sentence.

Also, the fact that Barnabas felt compelled to apologize for someone who was not present at the table was not unexpected but demonstrates how powerful Whiteness is as an affect. As Teunis (2007) revealed in his study among White gay men, even just the mere mention of racism or racialization processes garnered violent reactions from his White informants, who felt it to be an accusatory frame. Many of my participants have responded to racism like Barnabas, including myself in other situations, in trying to appease an imaginary White subject who was not physically present, but was **still** present at all our *talanoa*.

Korean sons return home

Barnabas: Everyone on my mother's side has passed away except my mum's eldest. All her cousins came. So, Joseph [alias] is the Chinese one; he's a good-looking kid, and everyone was like: "Oh, he's the Park!" So, he instantly gets $100, and then they look at Sarah [alias], she has got green eyes, dark skinned, she's not thin, they looked at her and were like, "too fat; too dark." I love Korea, they don't beat around the bush. The relatives were all ignoring Sarah, but she's half me. Everyone was also wearing visors, and Sarah asked me, "Why are they covering themselves?" I said to her, "It's because they value light skin," and then there comes my redhead, pasty white. And people's reactions were, "Your wife must be so white." […] I didn't say anything, mum was like, "yeah," she's working at home." Because my husband didn't come as well, he knew the drama and flaked out at the last minute.

This excerpt, which was shared in earlier chapter, is revisited here as a way to consider more intentionally the way race and racism plays out in the experiences of queerness shared by participants like Barnabas; experiences that move and shift as mobility in our contemporary context becomes much easier. In a transnational sense, this mobility is a movement that allows concepts to blur their geographical context, pulling Seattle and Seoul closer together. As explained earlier, Barnabas had returned to his birthplace two summers before our *talanoa* with his mother and children. Joseph was an adopted son, whilst Sarah was his biological daughter conceived through surrogacy. This lively tale he shared about how his extended family reacted to meeting his children for the first time upon returning to Korea demonstrates many features of Korean social norms and interpretive constructs of skin color. Joseph, an adopted son, embodied the desired aesthetics within Korean cultural norms. This crafted him as a more desirable family member aesthetically, and he received a real monetary reward. Meanwhile, Sarah, who was described as more plump and darker, was less desirable.

The commentary of how Sarah was startled to see people wearing visors, and the way Barnabas explained it to her, speaks to a Korean preference for White skin related historically to class (Li, Min, and Belk, 2008). In Korea, people who have white skin have long been told that they look noble. In the upper class of the Goryeo dynasty (918–1392), children washed their faces with peach flower water to make their skin clean, white, and transparent, and girls before marriage were desperate to have white skin (Li, Min, and Belk, 2008, p. 445). Furthermore, Barnabas' return to Korea brought with him a new positionality, in that his family made gendered assumptions modified by race; assumptions that his spouse, or presumed wife, was White. He storied this as a type of wonderment for his extended family that he and I laughed knowingly about. Yet, as a direct result of him living in the US, his children, and his mother's complicity in pushing this narrative of convenience, allowed him to navigate the complexity of a familial situation as a gay male in one moment by inadvertently drawing on a type of positionality constituted by the forces of racialization. In this case, it opened a moment of inclusion for him that orbited around Whiteness.

Moments of racialized inclusion for returned sons of Korea was a theme that continued in the responses of other Seattle participants. Over the year of fieldwork in Seattle, I came to know Reuben and his husband well. Often, we would meet for a meal or coffee to talk about how we were all, me included, adjusting to Seattle life. We spent one lovely afternoon in Green Lake on an early spring day, where I connected him and his husband to my other friends in Seattle who were a married gay couple. Reuben and his husband would also cook Korean food for me at their apartment, allowing me to participate in an expression of longing for a return to Korea that we storied as a collective memory. Although we had not known each other before meeting in Seattle, we had lived in Seoul at around the same time. Reuben was well aware of the issues of racialization and the process in which Koreans valorized Whiteness, and they featured a lot in our conversations as a result of my clearly racialized positionality. Having experienced it firsthand myself in Seoul, as alluded throughout this book, all participants inevitably gravitated toward the issue. For Reuben, when we spoke about his biracial status, he storied it as a type of advantage, something that gave him a competitive edge in the ultra-competitive job market in South Korea. But further to this, he also believed that this allowed him to enjoy better social interactions and create links within South Korea

Patrick: Do you think claiming an American identity in Korea affects the way other people interacted with you?

Reuben: Yeah, I think being a Westerner kind of comes with some level of prestige, especially being a native

English speaker, and especially being an American. Because Korea has so many ties with the US. And I think Americans are generally well-liked, it's one of the few places in the world where Americans are liked.

Patrick: What sort of prestige or privilege did it bring you?

Reuben: People want to be your friend more. People are nicer to you and their interactions are just nicer.

Patrick: Is this in comparison to other people's experiences?

Reuben: Yeah, I mean in comparison to other foreigners from like Southeast Asia and non-Western countries.

For Reuben, race, racism, and racialization are layered with additional complexity. For one thing, he is biracial. Whilst research that documents the experiences of biracial Korean Americans in the US is considerable (see Standen, 1996; Young, 2009 as examples), the literature that focuses on the experiences of biracial Korean Americans in South Korea is still developing. Ji Hyun Ahn's (2015) study on the rise of White mixed-race celebrities as a desired marker of Global Koreanness is an example of this. She concludes that mixed-raciality – White biraciality – is desired in order to imagine Korea as a global nation. In other words, unlike other types of racial/ethnic minorities such as migrant workers, Asian mixed-race people are often discussed under multiculturalism, while White biracial celebrities are deployed as a symbol of transnational mobility associated with global competence. Using the example of biracial Korean actor Daniel Henney, Ahn argues that, as a White mixed-race celebrity, Henney does not have to fight for cultural recognition or engage in a battle of "multicultural recognition" because Whiteness is already desirable and has cultural currency.

Reuben's positionality also suggests, supported by Ji Hyun Ahn's (2015) study, that biracial Koreans (half-White American) may be able to access certain privileges in Korea that may make their navigation of reverse-migration different than other returnee Koreans. In his White-American half, he believed that he found moments of racialized inclusion, where the centrality and symbolic power of Whiteness associated with Americans brings a more respected and liked identity point.

> I think the way Koreans don't separate nationality from race. For them, Korean is not just your nationality, it's your cultural identity, your race, it's your language, it's everything. So, I think when most Koreans think of Americans, they're thinking of White people; if they see that you're not White, they think you're not American.

Reuben's suggestion that Koreans did not consider anyone not White to be American is a broad sweep of a general sentiment and personal observation of the time. While this is not intended as a definitive critique, it does suggest a racialized image of Americans that often disqualifies non-White Americans from being considered as "fully" American. In positioning Whiteness as a central feature of how Koreans construct Americans, Reuben's narrative is brought in line with Incho Lee's (2011) work, which argued that Koreans positioned themselves in relation to Whiteness due to its proximity to prosperity associated with globalization. Reuben's earlier remarks about feeling more included and welcomed in Korea because of his American status finds parallels with Barnabas' experience as a returned son of Korea with one light-skinned child versus one with darker traits. Although, in Barnabas' case, the difference between how his children were treated may also be linked to the fact that his son looked like a "Park" – or in other words, more Korean. I argue that this is still a racialized construct, as was noted earlier: the lighter-skinned aesthetic is a desirable one related to class status in South Korea's construct and view of skin color. Therefore, his son's acceptance was subjected to a Korean form of racialization tied to perceived class status.

Discussion questions

Although this chapter has focused on race and racism experienced by Korean gay men, what are other aspects orbiting around the concept of race that mediates your own experiences in the context in which you live?

How important do you think race is to the way different men experience queer spaces in the city that you live in?

Considering Korea's own history around the preference for white skin, how much do local norms and constructs around race, versus transnational understandings, impact what Patrick was observing in Seattle?

What do you understand as being the function of race/racism in queer spaces and how does that color your interpretation of the insights shared in this chapter?

Note

12. In a study of dating preferences among Asian American gay men, Tsunokai et al. (2014) showed how Asian American men – despite being subjected to racial stereotypes that depicted them in ways often tied to effeminate behavior, with

small penises ripe for White consumption – still preferred dating White men above other groups. Phua (2007) also demonstrated how many of his Asian American participants preferred dating White gay men despite being subjected to racialization in the gay dating community.

7

Insidious collusion: Exploring the transnational nature of gay racism[13]

Patrick: Have you dated foreign guys before? If so, where are they from?

Seunghwa: America, America, England, Korean American, those were the serious ones. I have dated many people from European countries. Oh, and some Asian countries too. Taiwan, China; there was a Greek guy and an Australian. It depends on what you mean by "date"

Patrick: How you define dating, so if you consider it dating, we'll go with that. What about their ethnicity or race?

Seunghwa: White, but I'm not necessarily looking for White men. I also dated a half-Mexican, half-White guy.

Patrick: How do you usually meet them?

Seunghwa: Apps. Jack'd, Grindr, and Tinder.

Patrick: When you use these apps, what are the common types of foreigners that you come across?

Seunghwa: Koreans obviously, but then White Americans usually. I think it's because there are many English teachers and students. When it comes to English teaching jobs, I know they prefer White instructors, that's why.

Although most of my experiences of the city took place around my home in Itaewon, I had worked in Gangnam – Dogok-dong to be exact – and Gangdong-gu. While I was at graduate school at Seoul National University, I briefly lived in Sadang-dong, to be closer to the Gwanak campus. There was no denying that anywhere you went in Seoul, White foreigners were very visible. They stood out from crowds that we would all get lost in as we pursued our next transit point. I, at least, had soft, Samoan features that could be mistaken as Asian in certain light, allowing me to blend in when I styled my clothing to follow the trend of the day. But for the most part, you could always tell a White foreigner from America. For participants like Seunghwa, there were many modes in which they came into contact with White foreigners. In the previous excerpt, Seunghwa details his experiences of dating mostly White foreigners and predominantly English teachers. These English teachers from outside Korea became one of the most common ways participants storied their initial experiences with foreigners, and especially with White foreigners.

Sam, one of the Seoul participants, giggled as he explained to me how he had a huge crush on his English teacher in high school. He said the teacher was a White man from New Zealand and absolutely loved the accent. He blushed as he told me that he had once fantasized about him as he came to understand his own growing queer desire. All participants in Seoul, including those who had never left Korea, had all at some stage dated a White man. These men that they dated were most likely from one of the seven countries identified as native English-speaking countries under Korean immigration law. These countries are the US, UK, Ireland, Canada, Australia, South Africa, and New Zealand. Only citizens from these countries, at the time, were allowed to apply for an E-2 visa, or a visa that allows for someone to be employed as a native English teacher in South Korea. This separate visa class also created a racialized inflection around the type of foreigners from these nations that participants were likely to encounter.

> There are more White guys here than Black guys. Out of all the foreigners in Korea, they're mostly White guys, even more than other Asians in Seoul. Southeast Asians are more like kinda factory workers, so they don't live in Seoul. They live in rural areas. But for me it's not about that. It's whether they can hold a conversation. I can hook up with any guy. [...] I don't think I have a special thing for White guys, but I date White guys.

For Soonchang, his interpretation for the higher probability of dating White men relates to their relative number and proximity in Seoul. Soonchang's insight here is pertinent, as he understands his dating patterns in relation to the way the city is racially spatialized, in that White men are just more likely to be in Seoul because of the work many are allowed to engage in (teaching) versus migrants from Southeast Asia who are more likely to be factory workers. This interpretation is consistent with work carried out by Korean scholars, who argue that Korea's foreigner community is split between a professional elite and the "low-skilled" migrant class (Seol, 2012), and, as a result, is geographically bound and separated across the cityscape. Soonchang is referring here to how Gyeonggi-do, the province surrounding metropolitan Seoul, is full of factories, working as the engine room of Korean manufacturing. This province is often the landing place of many Southeast Asian migrants, whilst the urban, cosmopolitan hub of inner Seoul is the playground of middle-class migrant English teachers and professionals often from countries participants described as the West. What is significant is that in Soonchang's *talanoa,* the racialized impacts of this structural design can be read as a mediator to how he, a Korean gay man, is able to explore his own dating and sexuality desire. In many ways Soonchang was just "playing the field" when he ended up dating predominantly White men. That was the type of man he was most likely to encounter.

For Sam, however, it was not as simple as just "playing the field." He had relayed that he struggled with dating Koreans, unlike YG in Seattle who only dated Korean. Sam did not see any type of futurity for gay marriage in South Korea. As such, Korean gay men were less likely to want to engage in the long-term relationship that he craved, as was intimated in earlier chapters. When I asked him whether he felt there was a racial preference among the gay community in Korea, as was beginning to emerge in *talanoa* with other participants like Soonchang, he was emphatic in his response.

> Korean gays are racist: they prefer White guys. I think it's possible you've experienced that, but I'm not sure if you've seen it. They don't want to date anyone who is from Southeast Asia and they don't really like Brown guys much unless they're Latino.

Sam, who was living in Seoul and had never lived abroad, importantly, stories racism within the Korean community toward foreigners as hierarchized, where not all foreigners are treated the same. For him, White sits at the apex, and othered brown bodies are constructed as undesirable, unless they are Latino. This eerily mirrors racialization patterns found in studies conducted in the US among Asian American gay men, where there is a strong preference for the White gay male, whilst other brown bodies are subjected to different standards of aesthetic value (Phua, 2007; Tsunokai, McGrath, and Kavanagh, 2014), inferring some sort of connection in the racialized practices between the two locations. In doing so, Sam uses the term "they" to refer to Koreans, which suggests that in some way he may have been trying to distance himself from this racialized practice. His questioning of me about my own experiences represents a felt-knowing that Sam instinctively thought I could relate to, as a Brown researcher with several years of living in Seoul. Later, Sam was careful to emphasize that his only boyfriend at that moment in time had been Brown, despite having dated White guys in the past.

Martin's first ever boyfriend was a White American English teacher. And his explanation of the racialized preference in dating that existed within the Korean gay community related to wider Korean social structures and views of race. In detailing this hierarchy, he also introduced a friend from Malaysia who said they loved Korea, but had also experienced embarrassing forms of racism from Korean gay men. As he was speaking with a Brown researcher in this space, I could feel that he felt compelled to apologize, as I'm sure he, much like Sam, suspected that I would be able to relate.

> One of my gay friends from Malaysia, he loves Korea, but he has had many bad experiences with Korean gay guys: racist experiences. It makes me feel awful. In Korea, there is rank related to race. Koreans come first, second would be Japanese, third are White Westerners or Taiwanese, and after that all colored people are the same. In my experience that is how people think. It's not just gay people, it's across the board. If you're a Korean parent, it goes: Korean, Japanese, White Westerner, maybe Chinese is OK; except that, they don't like anyone else.

Martin's explanation ties racism within the gay community in Korea directly to societal-wide racialization processes. Here he uses the desires of parents around marriage as a way to apprehend the racial hierarchies in desire that have transmitted into the Korean gay community. Moreover, by stratifying the dating preferences into the desire of specific gay bodies, he adds a structural nuance to what Sam had offered by positing that Korean gay men prefer Japanese men above Westerners. This is an important idea, as literature on Korean society has described how, when Koreans marry outside of the Korean race, it is preferred that their sons married women from countries who demonstrated the ability to easily assimilate into Korean life both culturally and aesthetically (Kim, 2011). However, even in Martin's explanation, White gay men were still given a special category of their own. They were included as an acceptable other, whilst everyone else was considered unsalvageable.

When I spoke with Gene about his experiences of dating with foreigners, he shared similar sentiments as Sam, taking an accusatory tone toward the racially inflected desires of Korean gay men. Gene was also critical of this practice, yet was still a participant, co-opted into this scheme of desire; he offered this toward the end of our *talanoa*.

Patrick: Do you have any preference to the type of guys you prefer to date?

Gene: Westerner with a good personality. I need to find many things in common. He should drink and enjoy going out. I prefer bigger and taller guys than me.

Patrick: Which ethnicity have you dated before?

Gene: White.

Patrick: When using apps here in Korea, what kind of foreigners do you come across?

Gene: Mostly White, but I've seen some Asians and Latinos.

Patrick: Do you have a preference?

Gene: White and Latino.

Patrick: I think that's about it, is there anything else you want to add that I may have missed? Thoughts about gay life in Korea?

Gene: In Korea, gay society is really small, especially in Itaewon. We all know each other. I can know who they are, or who their ex-boyfriend is. So bad rumors can follow you. I've met a lot of exchange students and they're kind of like playboys, you know. They're here for a short time and have fun, then leave. Especially White, as they are popular here in Korea, so they are very rude and not polite.

Patrick: Do you believe that White gay men are treated better in Korean society?

Gene: Yes, I found Korean society very racist because we prefer White people. I have a Filipino American friend and he was rejected as a native speaker teacher in Korea because of his ethnicity.

Our candid exchange bore the hallmarks of racialized inflections, and I continued to sense participants' shifting our *talanoa* to race knowingly, as my positionality loomed large in this space. As a result, Gene highlights how the process of racialization in the gay community is something that all participants were acutely aware of and wanted to speak about. What marked Gene out from other participants was how he never sought to distance himself from racialized dating patterns. In acknowledging that he did have a racial preference in the way he dated, he was highlighting his role in the racialization process that he was complicit in reproducing. Karen Pyke (2010) talks about how internalized racism and its contribution to the reproduction of racial inequality has been largely ignored and is problematic. She argues that only by defying this taboo will we be able to expose the hidden mechanisms that sustain White privilege. Gene's acknowledgement is important, as he demonstrates how racialization works insidiously to co-opt even racialized subjects.

In structures that uphold racism, we are all implicated, even as allies (Gordon, 2005).

Utilizing the foreigner construct as point of reference

For some participants, having foreigner friends brought other advantages. The first advantage was that for participants involved in queer activism, foreign friends' proximity to Western liberation discourses gave them access to discursive practices that could be used to challenge the heteronormativity and heterosexism that pervaded Korean society in their experience. The second advantage was when it came to finding support in navigating coming out, considering the lack of reference points that existed in South Korea at the time.

Hank, one of the participants introduced in the previous chapter, had risen in the mid-2010s to become one of the Seoul gay community's most well-known performers and activists. Born and raised in South Korea, Hank is a regular at gay Pride festivals all over the country, and we had known each other for some time on the scene. He also runs quite a prominent online group dedicated to highlighting the complexities of gay life in Korea. His group aims to bridge the gap between Koreans and foreigners in South Korea that exists often because of the language barrier. In this excerpt from his interview, he explains how his online group works and the role of foreign members in supporting the work of his group.

> **Hank:** My organization is the only one that I am part of now. There are some secret groups like "Gay Men in Seoul," "Gay People in Daegu," but I wanted to make

a public group and one that was nonprofit. I started with the couple hundred of my Facebook friends. In 2015 we had over 1,000 members and right now we have 5,600 people. It is growing very fast. I think it is playing a huge role in[the lives of] LGBT people in Korea because it's mainly for English speaking people. Because there are lot of bilingual Korean people, we can translate lots of articles and information. We've been the bridge between Korean LGBT community and foreign LGBT community.

Patrick: What sort of information have you been translating? English to Korean? Or Korean to English?

Hank: Both. We don't hire professional translators. Group members just voluntarily translate important articles from countries about legalizing gay marriage or issues regarding LGBT in Korea. So, for the most part, Koreans and non-Korean LGBT members can interact.

What this excerpt from Hank's *talanoa* demonstrates is that participants perceived foreigner connections as having brought them strength. By drawing on the possibilities of online connectedness in transnationally joining a gay assemblage of sorts, Hank uses the internet as an online community-building site capable of providing accessible and no-cost translation services, while developing pipelines of information to disseminate useful discourses aimed at establishing Korea's LGBT community within a wider global gay subjectivity.

In this way, I purport, for activists like Hank, that having foreigner friends and acquaintances represents an instrumental utility, related to attempts at reforming heteronormative erasure of gay identity in South Korea, through two mechanisms. The first is the material effect of free labor through volunteer translation services. The second, seen through a queer developmental citizenship lens as explained by Woori Han (2018), is the casting of Korea's position on queer rights as one that needed to catch up with the West to fully develop local ideas of citizenship to include and protect queer subjectivities. The reverse flow of information from these connections allowed Hank and other gay Korean men to talk back to the global community, showing the progress they were making. In doing so, Hank can story the development of tolerance for LGBT people and develop a teleological and progressing narrative of South Korean gay life attempting to transform itself into becoming more like the West on queer issues.

Getting a little help to come out in Seoul

In addition, for Hank, having foreigner friends and being enmeshed within a foreigner community was particularly important as he began to develop his own desire to declare his identity as a gay male. He explained how he had decided to come out to his mother as gay. And he described how part of what made him comfortable enough to do this was the embeddedness within social communities that he described as being more Westernized. This allowed him to create kinship ties with foreign friends he considered to be his community in Seoul.

> **Patrick:** You told me that you have come out. Can you tell me more about it?

Hank: It was in 2013 and back then, after graduating from Korean high school, I didn't hang out with Korean friends, partly because of my sexuality and what I wanted to do. It's hard to achieve that around typical Korean men. I started to make new friends who studied abroad, and Korean Americans. And even with complete foreigners. By 2013, most of my friends were not conservative and [were] Westernized. I didn't have to hide my sexuality to them. So, all my friends knew about my sexuality. At that time, I decided to come out to my family in 2013. I didn't want to do it alone, so I brought my best gay friend who's from Israel. He was just there with me for the whole time. I asked my Mom to come to a coffee shop and came out there.

Patrick: How did your mother react, if you don't mind me asking?

Hank: She was very calm. She was surprised but she was OK with it. She knew I had a lot of gay friends. She watched a lot of Western movies and shows. She was comfortable with the idea of gay and everything. Later that night, she texted to me that it is OK to be gay and she still loves me. Maybe a few months later, my mom told my sister and sister also texted me that she also supports me.

Hank's coming out story involves the role of foreigners as reference points in helping to facilitate new kinships in navigating familial relationships. Hank, throughout his development of a gay identity, drew on the divide between Korean conservatism and perceived foreign progressiveness over sexual identity to make sense of his own marginality. By grounding himself among a foreign community, he appears to have found a source of strength that allowed him to confront the prospect of having to try and negotiate his relationship with his mother as a gay son. Taking his Israeli friend with him to his coming-out story may have also contributed to the sense of neutrality that the coffee shop, as a venue for his coming-out, provided. In both these ways, he was able to draw on the foreigner construct as other, to help him achieve the successful negotiation of a new kinship relationship.

Additionally, Hank interpreted his mother's own reactions to be mediated by her exposure to Western movies and shows and her pre-exposure to his gay friends. This echoes many comments made by participants in earlier chapters regarding the role Western media played in helping to shape articulations of queerness among participants in Seoul. In many ways, Hank suggested, for his successful renegotiation of his position within the family of son to gay son, reference points for his family members were also important. Having positively reinforcing reference points for both was key to helping him succeed in coming out and smoothing over relations with his own family. For both, foreigners were the source of these reference points.

Managing the realities of the language barrier in queer spaces

However, in other contexts, foreigners were not seen as an advantage. As alluded to by Gene, pre-COVID, there had been a massive influx of international students to South Korea. There were 12,000 were studying in South Korea in 2003, and 123,850 in 2018 (Chung, 2018). Many of these students have joined LGBT clubs at their Korean universities. A member of the Seoul National University LGBT club who spoke to me during my fieldwork explained that, since I had studied there, the club had grown but had fractured somewhat. It now had a dual membership structure. There was an LGBT club for Koreans, and an LGBT club for foreigners. This split was common in universities that had many foreign students, and, as Martin explained, was related to the issue of language. Where Hank had found utility in building connections with foreigners online, and in gaining support for his coming-out story, some LGBT clubs in Korea found having foreigners as members of their clubs was at times a hindrance. Martin was the former president of his university's LGBT club at one of Korea's SKY group of universities. The SKY universities, consisting of Seoul National, Korea, and Yonsei Universities, are considered Korea's elite three (Choi, Calero, and Escardíbul, 2012).

> **Martin:** I went to their homecoming party, there were so many international students; there was even a separate section for international students. Korean universities have so many international exchange students now, so the gay clubs got so much bigger.

> **Patrick:** I heard that some LGBT clubs in Korea now have a separate club for international students and a separate one for Korean students. That's what happened at my old university.

> **Martin:** Yeah, that's because if you want to unite them, you'd have to make bilingual materials, and that's difficult and time consuming.

What this suggests, then, is that gay foreigners' inclusion into the structures of Korean gay life is contextual and can be based on moments of their perceived value and utility to Korean gay men. These conditions are complex and story the multiple effects and outcomes that the processes that undergird racialized modernity produce. Conditional imbrication can be read through a utilitarian lens we are familiar with in the West and can be found reproducing in the South Korean context.

White gay men and the cooptation of racialization narratives

Michael: Koreans are racist, and homophobic. You know, this society has a long way to go with that sort of thing. I mean, it's changing, but in general I experience racism here a lot. On public transport, people don't want to sit next to you cause you're a foreigner. It can get annoying fast, I mean even at my job. I speak good Korean, but they insist on speaking broken English to me. But they don't do it to my other co-workers who are Asian and speak Korean, when my Korean is better than theirs.

As Michael, a White American male, retold his account of experiencing racial prejudice in South Korea, I sat alongside him in a Seoul bar among a group of five around a low-set table. Michael was a "professional worker;" he was tall, blonde, and blue eyed. He had studied in Korea in the past and had lived in Korea for a considerably shorter period than I had. That night, our table included three Korean gay men who were my friends. The three Koreans in our party nodded at Michael in sympathy, occasionally interjecting with offers of acknowledgement and comments that supported his characterization of Korean society's tendency to treat foreigners differently. Throughout the entire interaction, Michael not once acknowledged the way in which foreigners of different ethnic and national backgrounds experienced racialization differently. When I suggested that migrant workers in South Korea from South and Southeast Asia may be treated worse than we middle-class professional workers due to the nature of the industries they are employed in, he brushed it off saying "I can't speak to that experience," and continued for a lengthy period explaining his experiences of exclusion.

Although he did not deny that differences existed between his experience and that of non-White foreigners in South Korea, by continuing to speak on his experience whilst refusing to interrogate the differences in positionality he enjoyed as a White man, he not only centered himself, but was complicit in the racialization of others. In fact, as I sat there, a clearly Brown body, and after about 15 minutes of his confessional monologue, I realized that his lived experience was a topic of conversation he was trying to draw me into as well. He repeatedly paused and looked in my direction after presenting anecdotes of his experiences of racialized exclusion. In those moments, it became apparent that he was attempting to build a narrative bridge between the two of us as foreigners, inviting me to comment. Eventually, I obliged, offering anecdotes of my own experiences of racialization to ensure he did not feel alone in the conversation. Later, I wrote in my researcher diary that I was unsure whether I had participated as a type of catharsis – which I also noted was highly unlikely, considering I had made peace with my racialized status in South Korea long ago – or whether it was to offer Michael support. I later concluded that it was the latter. Throughout the conversation, I was selective in what I presented, aware of the group mood; I did not offer any of the examples of when I had experienced racism from White men in South Korea, so as to not offend him and risk bringing the social interaction into an uncomfortable space.

The process I just storied is an example of how complex the effects and forces of racialization are when a White gay man navigates race from the position of racializer, whilst claiming the positionality of a victim, in the presence of BIPOC within the foreigner community in South Korea. According to Allan Bérubé (2001), this is one way in which gay stays White, where White gay men with the most visibility and power in the gay community stay silent on the racialization process of others, whilst simultaneously centering their own experiences of marginalization. In this situation, we can see that Michael, by virtue of his position as a White man in South Korea who occupies a racially privileged position within the foreigner community, also possesses the power to cast himself as a victim of racism due to South Korea's own structures and processes of racialization. For Michael, because he is a victim of racism, empathy for other victims of racism is merely optional. At the same time, for racialized subjects who have their skin color coded, it is a mandatory marker of their social positionality.

Foreigners living in South Korea are constituted in and racialized in different ways; ways that are arranged hierarchically, as documented by participants in their own stories. However, all those who are not Korean are represented discursively in a singular way: as foreigners. At the time I conducted my research (2016–2018), Statistics Korea (2018) reported that foreigners made up 2.9% of the population, with nearly 49% of those being Chinese nationals, including Chinese-Koreans (33.6%). Vietnamese made up 10%, Thais 6.3%, and the rest were categorized as "others" at 35.7%. The total foreigner population was just under 1.5 million. For Americans in particular, there are two main entry points: through the military, where there are approximately 28,500 military personnel; and as professional workers, mainly English teachers. However, there is no distinction made in any of these statistics around ethnic or racial difference intra-nationally. For one thing, the ethnic diversity that exists within countries like the US, and even my context of New Zealand, is effectively erased. No dataset currently exists in South Korea that looks at the ethnic breakdown of foreigners who come from the "big seven," carrying multiple national or ethnic affiliations.

Therefore, the process of valorizing Whiteness in South Korea as the dominant image of a Westerner has not been systematically interrogated for its own discursively erasive modality in this context. This was recognized by some foreign gay BIPOC whom I encountered over the course of my fieldwork in Seoul. When I met James, he was working as an English teacher. James was Filipino American and had found it difficult to date Koreans due to what he called their "racialized images of Westerners." But further to that, he had found that it was often difficult for him to find work in comparison to his White American friends. This excerpt is from our conversation one evening in Itaewon after an event that I had hosted for Pacific people in Seoul.

James: Yeah, Korean guys are way more into White dudes, you know, the frat types. Them, they usually look down on guys like me 'cause they think I'm just Filipino, and they just don't seem to like people from Southeast Asia. It's that whole from-a-poor-country bias thing that Koreans have. But it's also even when they're hiring for English teaching jobs, they prefer White teachers.

Patrick: I have heard stories like that too from some of my friends, and I was also turned down for an English teaching job for the same reason. They literally told me after the interview that they really liked me, but the parents wanted a White teacher.

James: That happened to one of my friends as well. But you kind of just get used to it coz that's life here, I guess.

Patrick: Yeah, I know, I'm over it. I mean, not in a bad way; over it in the sense that there are other things I love about living here, and let's be honest, there are issues to do with race that our own countries haven't yet figured out, so I give Korea a much wider berth than my own country considering Korea's limited experience with ethnic diversity.

James: I feel the same way. I love it here despite all these problems. I have some amazing Korean friends who are like family to me as well. So, I don't even think about it until something happens.

After our interaction, I realized that what James and I had engaged in was a type of rationalization of marginality that negotiated our relative exclusions from a racialized lens in the context of

Korean realities. But in giving a free-pass in this way, we were in effect allowing the re-inscription and centering of Whiteness at the apex of the racial hierarchy in the South Korean foreigner construct to continue. Critical race theory argues that in order to challenge the uneven textures of racialized modernity, BIPOC and other marginalized people can make use of counter-narratives to talk back against the dominance of White scripts that discursively construct us as racialized others (Delgado and Stefancic, 2017; Han, 2007, 2008b, 2008a). In many ways, it was what James and I had engaged in. However, even in counter-narratives, the White hegemonic narrative is still the core target and remains centered. It was as Gordon (2005) postulated: we were also implicated in the perpetuation of Whiteness being positioned as the center, as our narratives continued to orbit around it as a referential.

Greg was a White gay male from the Midwest US who had contacted me via a dating app. At first, he had seen my profile and broached the idea of perhaps going out on a date with me, but I made it clear that I was not particularly interested in dating anyone while doing fieldwork for my dissertation. Hence, we ended up becoming friends over the course of my time in Seoul. We met regularly for coffee and chats about life as foreigners in Korea. Unlike Michael, who was introduced at the beginning of this section, Greg found nuance in his discussions with me when the issue of race was brought up. In navigating the topic, he acknowledged the differences between our experiences. Despite being in Korea for a much shorter period, he explained that he had experienced multiple forms of racialized exclusion.

> **Greg:**   Ugh, it's hard here sometimes living as a foreigner, being excluded all the time, the way people talk about

you, especially in Korean, when you can understand Korean. But when my Korean wasn't so good, people would treat me like, "you're stupid because you're not able to speak Korean well." But, you know, everyone who's here on a teaching visa has at least got a degree.

Patrick: Well, that doesn't exactly make you smart either. Having a degree, especially in Korea where nearly everyone has them.

Greg: Right, but also, they look down on English teachers here for some reason. I feel that a lot, it's like they think we're just here to drink and party and commit crimes all the time. Remember how everyone keeps bringing up that pedophile case, and that all foreigners have AIDS and are child molesters. But, you know what, I can't imagine what it must be like to be a PoC in Korea, having that prejudice against you, plus experiencing racism in your own country too. I imagine it must be way worse than what I experience here. But you're from New Zealand, so it might be different than America.

Patrick: It's definitely different, I mean, the whole foreigners as child molesters and carriers of AIDS I'm aware of, but it's not really the first thing I think of when someone mentions racism in Korea. I tend to think more of the racism in hiring practices among employers that favor White teachers, and the favorability of the White aesthetic and Korean beauty cosmetics industries. But yeah, coming from New Zealand, racism definitely exists there, don't worry.

Greg: Ahhh, that's interesting. But also, that's where we are
        different because I don't have to deal with any of that.
        That's my privilege.

Short of Korean society driving discursive shifts around
understanding the full textures of White privilege and neoliberal
currency of capital within their own structures and hierarchies
of power, counter-narratives told by BIPOC in the Korean gay
community, even when acknowledged by White gay men,
will still struggle to shift attitudes and queer practices that do
not center Whiteness and its symbolic value as a productive
modality. I offer this assertion not only because of the allure of
Whiteness as symbolic power, but due to the transnationally
linked relationship of the structures that facilitate its flow within
the local gay community. In Seoul, as outlined by participants
and experienced firsthand through my own years there, the gay
community is small and relatively hidden.

Despite this isolation, participants recalled incidences of racial
discrimination that they struggled against in some moments and
resisted in others, but ultimately impacted the way they navigated
gay cross-cultural and inter-racial dating. As a globalizing discourse
around a universal gay identity that seeks liberation from barbaric
and backward cultural formations continues to assert itself today,
South Korea's gay queer communities are protectors of their own
local expressions and formations of queerness. However, without
the centering of this reflexive turn, their own practices can fall
prey to the machinations of neocolonial scripts hidden within
global ideas of universalizing gay identities that collude with the
South Korean state's own neoliberal biopolitical projects. In South
Korea, the influx of foreigners is highly regulated and predicated

on notions of citizenship and one's membership into particular nations that South Korean society then arrange by class divisions. Richer Western countries are given a higher position by virtue of their proximity to prosperity in global historical narratives. This is a situation that can be clearly seen in the narratives of participants in this study.

Discussion questions

What are some of the ways that structural forms of racism in different societies (South Korea and the US) are converging in the stories of participants in Seoul?

This chapter has briefly touched on the role of language in shaping social interactions in queer spaces in Korea; how do you think this role is reflected in contexts like your own?

What do you make of White gay men claiming a position of racialized other in Seoul? How do you think our tools around race theory and transnationalism can help us unpack some of these complexities?

Considering the two contexts (Seattle and Seoul) covered in this book, what can be said about the role of race in the way we think about transnational subjectivities that compel us toward a universal queer utopia through queer politics?

How has the way Patrick's positionality impacted and made possible the types of insights he's shared in this book as a Samoan fa'afafine gay man?

Note

13. Portions of this chapter have been repurposed from my journal article published in the *Du Bois Review*, cited here as: Thomsen, P.S. (2020) 'Transnational Interest Convergence

and Global Korea at the Edge of Race and Queer Experiences: A Talanoa with Gay Men in Seoul', *Du Bois Review*: Social Science Research on Race, pp. 1–18. Available at: https://doi.org/10.1017/S1742058X20000247. I'd like to thank the editors of the Du Bois Review for publishing my article and Cambridge University Press for giving me permission to reproduce some of the work in this chapter and book.

8
Conclusion: Thoughts and reflections from a Samoan queer researcher

I once wrote in a publication that being gay is difficult anywhere, but being gay in Korea is downright dangerous. When I wrote that column shortly after my return to New Zealand, COVID had forced all of us into lockdown, and I was starting to gain some distance between this research and my memories over a decade of living in environments and contexts that were not my own. As I reflect upon what this research represents, I have no real desire to offer up a neat package, with the jagged edges trimmed off to represent tidiness in an elegantly crafted argument. Complexity sits at the heart of participant worlds.

In the pages of this book, I have not sought to offer a definitive representation of gay life for Korean gay men in Seattle and Seoul; as a Samoan and outsider to Korean culture and society, I think Korean queer researchers are the only ones who could even attempt such an ambitious task. Rather, what I hope I have achieved in these pages is the ability to show you the layered complexity of what being gay in the Korean context looked like for someone like me at this juncture of history. I was a Samoan New Zealander drawn to Korea out of economic necessity, subsequently thrown into an environment where I, too, had to grapple with issues that went beyond my citizenship and the cosmopolitan credentials that facilitated my movement to South Korea.

In 2008, I may have moved into a Korean society that was still figuring out how to talk about gay men and queer communities openly, but I was to find that issues of race and concepts of culture quickly foregrounded long histories tied to the contested and brutalized land of the Korean Peninsula. And this simple fact could not be divorced from any social research that I wished to contribute to discussions on experiences of marginalization in Korea. Thus, my sense of queerness and understanding of queerness and gay life in Korea was necessarily refracted through this complicated lens. Yet, the critiques and examinations of Korea's queer worlds I had heard, seen, and read, up until the point I began this research as a doctoral student, were often read through a Korea-West binary; a binary which Korean studies critical scholars I met along the way understood to be incomplete in capturing the full richness, contradictions, complexities, and possibilities around the practices of queerness that existed in Korea at the time of my coming of age.

As a Samoan who had grown up in New Zealand among the diaspora, I had spent many years traveling between both my ancestral home and my settler society. Experiences of racism in New Zealand made me acutely aware of how race, racism, and racialization were forces and processes that were slippery to grasp, hidden behind structures that obfuscated their roles in shaping experiences and engagements with one's everyday life and sexuality. But they were forces and processes that I could always **feel** and **sense** in moments of ordinary innocence. Although I began this project asking questions about what factors impacted decisions around coming out and visibility for Korean gay men, what I was privileged to end up with as a final body of work is a complex set of experiences lined with brittle edges, woven tightly and loosely in certain places, underpinned by narratives that traversed the great Pacific Ocean, crossing cultural boundaries and racial, transnational, and diasporic ties; offering a complex reading of globality and articulations of racialized and queer forms of modernity. My work forced me to grapple with the complex layers of another type of mobility beyond the pathways I was familiar with in the South Pacific.

The book opened with a recollection of my research encounters with Korean gay men in the great city of Seattle, and posed a simple question: what factors impacted the way that Korean gay men resident in Korea understood their own stories of coming out? Although existing literature at the time spoke about the way Korean gay life, even in the US, was governed by heterosexist social and cultural norms, participants storied a complex process of negotiation that included strategizing and enacting constructed performances of heteronormativity as methods to navigate these complicated structures. These included the power of the KACC as sites of community building and norm setting within the Korean American community. Narratives of convenience, although known by other names in other research traditions, and a concept I've argued in other publications, were deployed as an adaptive strategy to negotiate the complex coalescence of culture, Christianity, and migration. These are factors that massively impacted practices of queerness and identity-making in the lives of participants.

Most participants that I encountered in Seattle who were not born in the US chose to distance themselves from the Korean American community because of the exclusionary nature of the discourses that were formed around a gay identity. Moreover, it quickly became apparent that the fact that their families were not in the US meant that they were able to step into an American world, where they could live as gay men but continue to keep their sexual identity secret from their families in Korea. Thus, the Pacific Ocean became their ally in allowing them to deploy their own narrative of convenience. It was something my ex-boyfriend and his Korean gay friends had done. They lived openly as gay men in Seattle outside the Korean American community, and the physical division from their families in South Korea allowed them to keep their family safe; safe in the sense that any tensions that would emerge if their sexual identity were to be revealed in South Korea could be avoided. And although I do not use the concept of a narrative of convenience to frame the experiences of Korean gay men in Seoul as assertively as in Seattle, my decision here to highlight the familial space on my return to Korea displays a commonality in this strategy, which dovetails neatly into the way negotiated futurities were spoken about by Seoul participants.

Chapter 3's findings urge those of us undertaking research that seeks to understand transnational movements of people and cultures within the framework of Global studies to think in a less linear manner regarding time. We can do so by thinking not just about how engagements with culture can take place in separate geographical contexts, but also how these transnational locations can become re-sutured to a different temporal context facilitated by a cultural affinity. The fact that Korean American society and spaces have been shaped by a reference to Korean society that existed at a very different temporal incision in contemporary Korean history meant that, in the moment in which I encountered participants in Seattle, Korean gay men were meeting a reflection of their home that they believe had long passed. This caused them to remove themselves from fully participating in Korean society in the US, as participants believed they carried much more progressive values than those that Koreans in America were espousing. This inverts an Orientalist frame that often condemns locations in Asia as progress-less when framing local forms of queer life.

Participants in the study who grew up in the US were also aware of this transnational diasporic time warp, but from a different perspective. Their engagement with this conservatism came from within, and their existence sought to challenge this, embedding differences between Korean gay men that I encountered in Seattle, and suggesting that there wasn't just one way to be Korean in the US, much like there isn't just one way to be Samoan in the New Zealand context I know well. And why should there be, when at its edges, culture as a defining identity structure always begins to fray when stretched beyond our own geographic and situated contexts, offering us other ways to know ourselves again.

These lessons I learned in Seattle ultimately reshaped questions I would ask potential participants when I undertook my journey back to the city of Seoul. Namely, on my return, there was no longer a sense of disconnection between places. Rather, threads I had started to recognize in Seattle began to tug at me in Seoul, helping me to think through transnational queer mobilities as a set of entangled experiences that disrupted temporality and essentialist ideas around sexuality. Specifically, pulling on the thread of racialized experiences in reference to familial and cultural values/expectations allowed me to bring in my own experiences – those of a displaced Samoan – as a lens to give life to stories beyond theories that sorted and categorized experiences into distinctly dichotomous variables of study. My return to Seoul allowed me to see the way subjectivity in the gay and queer space was being constituted and made visible through different sets of logics. Culture and family, yes, but by rendering myself visible as a racialized researcher in the process, I could develop insights that also drew in understandings of the mutually constitutive pressure of race and sexuality within an environment and country whose contemporary structures formed in reference to American empire.

Take, for instance, the element of negotiated queer futurities in the narratives shared by participants in Seoul. Also, the exploration of *Chaggi Kwalli*, or self-reliance, in elements of this book: a concept that redirects and repurposes neoliberal logics of subjectivity tied to Korea's own story of rapid economic and social transformation. My encounters in Seoul continued to show that the concept and institution of family still looms large in the way participants narrated their life experiences. But the sense that queerness or gayness or homosexuality represented an existential threat, thus a stumbling block for inclusion, was problematized by participants. They told stories of a queer futurity or possibility that included potential acceptance and inclusion. Drawing on four forms of Korean familism this book has engaged with, exclusion and expulsion from the family was not simply taken as inevitable by participants if or when choosing to come out. Rather, they storied the Korean family as a place where individual positionality could be renegotiated even within a framework of collective, relational identity-making. Again, this calls into question our tendency to attach descriptors to verbs and nouns along hard binaries of positions that do not account for possibility and futurity. Seoul participants I encountered did not find themselves severing connections in their own queer and gay praxis. Instead, they saw their families as integral to their sense of self and subjectivity. The participants presented innovative ways to think through how continuing existing connections and relationships can be a way to move toward a queer futurity that does not sacrifice genealogy.

This observation does not in any way detract from the trauma that from many Korean gay men, and other members of queer communities in Korea, carry from experiences of exclusion from those they share genealogy with. The very existence of the Seoul queer shelter is testament to an experience that does not end in nuance and familial inclusion. Pain and trauma were indeed a feature of many of my conversations in both Seattle and Seoul, which I have sought not to reproduce in spectacular ways here for various reasons. Complexity is foregrounded here, and it sits at the heart of this book. I believe that our traumas as members of various marginalized communities have been the subject of much voyeurism that can easily slip into colonial and heterosexist logics. Because of this, I have chosen to emphasize complicated and layered conversations around multiple converging marginalizations, which include (perhaps as a result of my own biases as a researcher) the way queer subjects are made visible through the lens of race.

In both Seoul and Seattle, participants were both constituted as racialized and racializing subjects; a process of racialization that orbits around Whiteness as an affective aesthetic both in terms of desire and as a structuring force. Seattle participants experienced overt forms of racism from members of the public while interacting with others around them. The multiple effects this racism produces have been well-covered in this book; when Barnabas, for example, was spat on by a homeless woman in Spokane because he was Asian. Barnabas also experienced racialization in his own home; Cain was simply told to move out by their White therapist when they were struggling to navigate the complexities of being gay and living as a Korean in Seattle. As Jasbir Puar explains, as an assemblage, the transnational gay does not accrete in linear time or within discrete histories, fields, or discourses. In other words, the moments of exclusion and inclusion experienced, produced, resisted, and reproduced by participants at various points of time in their own narratives are all part of the processes and manifestations of racialized modernity. As Puar further posits, homonationalism, or the examination of racializing affects, from this perspective is not merely an accusation or a synonym for gay racism. Instead, it is an analytic for apprehending the consequences of transnational movements and their successes around LGBT rights movements in particular (Puar, 2016).

I have also attempted to show, throughout this book, the way that intertwined conditions of racialized modernity that we live under can be apprehended through the purview of participant' narratives in specific and nuanced ways. For Seoul participants, racialization was encountered in the form of structured and embedded Whiteness as a product of ethno-nationalism, which they critiqued and tried to resist in certain moments but were complicit in upholding in others. An example of their dual role in this process lies in how many of the participants recognized the problematic contours of racialized hierarchies in Korean constructs of racial othering, especially when they had foreigner friends who were non-Korean BIPOC who explained to them their experiences of racism in Korea. Yet, at the same time, all participants who were dating foreigners were either with a White man or had been with a White foreigner as their main experience of dating with non-Koreans. In addition, they found moments where Whiteness and foreignness were useful and able to be deployed in their own lives. This became instrumental when they wanted to reform the homophobia they saw within Korea or when they wanted to access a reference point for a full coming-out narrative.

In this light, we see that Korea and the West have been constituted by Seoul participants in a dichotomous power configuration, where participants believed using the terminology of the West and the lessons from overseas offered LGBTQI+ activists and queer communities in South Korea a way forward. In doing so, another complication is added to Korea's post-democratization society, where the acceptance of a foreign idea as being more progressive must rely on the inscription of colonial logic, supposing the superiority of Western frameworks. At the very least, this suggests that there are different shades to the homonationalist project. The productive modality of these discourses and formations was circulated through Western films, television programs, and music, which all participants took to be important factors in exposing them to ideas that related to a gay identity. This sits in sharp contrast to my experience as a Samoan, where global normativities around queerness offer colonial erasure and misrepresentations of the uniquely local context in which our forms of gender-sex-sexuality divergence are culturally and geographically located. The impacts of homonationalist processes are diffuse and situated.

When Seattle participants traveled back to Korea, their proximity to Whiteness as members of the Korean diaspora provided them with a social advantage in different settings. As a biracial American, Reuben's positionality shifted, allowing him to be included in Korean society in ways that other foreigners did not have access to. He contrasted this with the experiences of his Thai friend who had been subjected to negative forms of racialization. For Barnabas, returning to Korea with children who embody different racialized aesthetics garnered uneven responses from his extended family that had real material effects. His son, who looked whiter and whom the family took to be more Korean, was literally rewarded with more money, while his daughter, who was darker and fuller in figure, was criticized for not complying with a strict Korean ideal beauty aesthetic: an aesthetic where Whiteness is also a central part of the construct.

All the while, White gay men continue to arrive in Seoul and take advantage of a type of positionality that they usually do not occupy in their home countries, one that places them as a racialized other. This is facilitated by a structural link established by South Korea's desire to position itself as a competitive actor in the global race toward transnational neoliberal forms of development. I have referred to this link as a type of insidious, racialized collusion. White gay men are more likely than gay men of other ethnic backgrounds to be traveling to South Korea as teachers, simply because there are more White gay men that qualify. In this way, our own processes of racialization are abetted by Korea's, in that the conversation about discrimination around these English teachers always center on how Koreans treat foreigners, and never mentions how, within our countries, racial discrimination and uneven distribution of qualifications is also racialized. These two latter factors make it more likely that White men and women are the representatives of our countries to South Korea, which plays into the South Korean construct of the foreigner and racial hierarchies. These White English teachers do not have any vested interest in interrogating their own role in the Korean racialization process. As a result, the White gay men who can take the positions of foreigners are able to position themselves as a disqualified racial group, documented by Wagner and Van Volkenburg (2012), whilst at same time still accessing White privilege in hiring processes, and even social interactions, that affords them ways to be treated better than other non-Koreans in South Korea's gay community. This collusion is another way in which Whiteness reproduces itself as a mechanism of power.

By keeping the strict rules that allow only people from native English-speaking countries to migrate to Korea to teach English, and by importing cheap labor specifically from "Browner" countries to lower end factory jobs, the South Korean state is racializing its foreign population. This is one way we can critique the racial textures and consequences of increased forms of globality located within notions of a universalizing gay and queer identity. The side-effect of all of this is that, in 2018, the process of racialization in South Korea was uneven among the professional class of foreigners, despite there being uniform patterns in the way it appears in the literature and popular discourse. The marginalized foreigner is mostly seen as the English teacher or the lowly-valued manual laborer; both narratives that are still relatively marginal to South Korean society. However, as the predominant narratives and discursive representatives of the foreigner community, the singularity in this narrative can easily elide the differences in experiences between White foreigners and their BIPOC colleagues in professional settings especially. The contours of exclusion, the specifics of these experiences and narratives, are glossed over as Whiteness continues to be centered, referenced, and ultimately desired by Korean society.

To close this book, I leave you with this excerpt from part of a *talanoa* I had toward the end of my fieldwork in Seoul. This excerpt shows, in some ways, the multiple manifestations and complexities involved in participant narratives, and how they are affected by racialization as an assemblage of transnational connections, affects, and flows across multiple locations. But, ultimately, what drove this work, and what drives all those around me living under the conditions of queer and racialized modernity, was a desire to be able to love. In many ways, my work as a researcher sits within this nexus of desiring to know a pathway to love, or to show my *alofa*, as it is known in Samoan. This has been a book on transnational queer times as embodied in the words of the gay men who bravely participated in this work and who I am forever indebted to as an emerging scholar. My love for all my participants is a result of my Samoan upbringing that teaches me that there is nothing greater to pursue and show in life than love. So, despite all the complexities and entanglements I have attempted to show through this book and research, these is nothing more powerful than love in this life, and queer worlds, like all worlds we are part of, is driven by a pursuit of love.

Silas: I usually date White guys because most guys who approach me are White guys. They are usually from Europe and America. They are very comfortable dating drag queens, too.

Patrick: So, you don't actively seek White people out, they just approach you. Also, do you think the LGBT foreign community might just be predominantly White here?

Silas: Yes.

Patrick: So then, it just becomes a case of what is in front of you right? Not something where it's just a fact that you only like to date White people.

Silas: I don't know. But, yes, Korea is welcoming of White people.

Patrick: Do you think that's just to do with preference? Korea has been said to have hierarchy of race with preference.

Silas: Yes. Absolutely. Just look even in hair salons, you'll never find a Black model in there.

Patrick: Why do you think that's the case? Is it because Korean culture just prefers Whiter people?

Silas: Yes. Korea has already got an obsession with pale skin.

Patrick: Do you think that ideal has also filtered down into the gay community?

Silas: Yes. When I came back from California, I wanted to become White. My friends even said I should use sun block. I think I started to care a lot more about my skin color when I came back to Korea.

Patrick: Well, I think we should all wear sunblock to take care of our skin [laughter]. Does it matter to you if your boyfriend is White?

Silas: No, I don't think so, I just want someone who gives cuddles. After all, we all just want someone to love.

Patrick: That, I absolutely agree with.

To all the incredible participants, "I Seoul U" and will never be able to thank you enough for everything you shared with me on this journey.

Figure 1: Picture of Seoul City Hall Square on the day my fieldwork for his research ended.

Figure 1: A picture of Seoul City Hall Square. There is a zebra crossing in the foreground with a police officer standing in the middle directing traffic. On the other side of the road in front of the square, people are milling around fountains of water spouting from the ground in front of a white sign in block letters that says: I SEOUL U, the slogan of the city of Seoul in 2018, when this picture was taken. Behind the sign is a colonial looking building with a concrete facade. This was the original Seoul City Hall, which is connected to a much larger modern building behind it that was a dome shaped glass exterior - this is the main part of the Seoul City Hall complex. Between the white sign and the buildings are a row of trees, some white tents and flags in the distance.

References

Abelmann, N., Park, S. J. and Hyunhee, K. (2013). On Their Own: Becoming Cosmopolitan Subjects Beyond College in South Korea. In: *Global Futures in East Asia Youth, Nation, and the New Economy in Uncertain Times*, pp. 100–126.

Acharya, A. (2004). How Ideas Spread: Whose Norms Matter? Norm Localization and Institutional Change in Asian Regionalism. *International Organization*, 58(2), pp. 239–275. doi:10.1017/S0020818304582024.

Ahn, J.-H. (2015). Desiring Biracial Whites: Cultural Consumption of White Mixed-Race Celebrities in South Korean Popular Media. *Media, Culture & Society*, 37(6), pp. 937–947. doi:10.1177/0163443715593050.

Anae, M. (2016). Teu Le Va: Samoan Relational Ethics. *Knowledge Cultures*, 4(3), pp. 117–130.

Archibald, J.-A. et al. eds. (2019). *Decolonizing Research: Indigenous Storywork as Methodology*. London, UK: ZED.

Ayoub, P. M. (2015). Contested Norms in New-adopter States: International Determinants of LGBT Rights Legislation. *European Journal of International Relations*, 21(2), pp. 293–322. doi:10.1177/1354066114543335.

Baker, D. L. (2016). The Impact of Christianity on Modern Korea: An Overview. *Acta Koreana*, 19(1), pp. 45–67. doi:10.18399/ACTA.2016.19.1.002.

Ball-Rokeach, S. J. and DeFleur, M. L. (1976). A Dependency Model of Mass-Media Effects. *Communication Research*, 3(1), pp. 3–21. doi:10.1177/009365027600300101.

Battles, K. and Hilton-Morrow, W. (2002). Gay Characters in Conventional Spaces: Will and Grace and the Situation Comedy Genre. *Critical Studies in Media Communication*, 19(1), pp. 87–105. doi:10.1080/07393180216553.

Bérubé, A. (2001). How Gay Stays White and What Kind of White It Stays. In: B. B. Rasmussen et al., eds., *The Making and Unmaking of Whiteness*. Durham: Duke University Press, pp. 234–265.

Bong, Y. D. (2008). The Gay Rights Movement in Democratizing Korea. *Korean Studies,* 32, pp. 86–103.

Bonilla-Silva, E. (2018). *Racism without Racists: Color-Blind Racism and the Persistence of Racial Inequality in America*. 5th ed. Lanham, MD: Rowman & Littlefield.

Bryman, A. (2016). *Social Research Methods*. 5th ed. Oxford: Oxford University Press.

Campbell, E. (2016). *South Korea's New Nationalism: The End of 'One Korea'?* First Forum Press.

Cass, Map. (1979). Homosexual Identity Formation: A Theoretical Model. *Journal of Homosexuality*, 4(3), pp. 219–235. doi:10.1300/J082v04n03_01.

Chan, C. S. (1992). Cultural Considerations in Counseling Asian American Lesbians and Gay Men. In: *Counseling Gay Men & Lesbians: Journey to the End of the Rainbow*. Alexandria, VA: American Association for Counseling and Development, pp. 115–124.

Chang, K. S. (2011). *South Korea Under Compressed Modernity: Familial Political Economy in Transition*. London: Routledge (Routledge advances in Korean studies, 19).

Chase, T. (2012). Problems of Publicity: Online Activism and Discussion of Same-Sex Sexuality in South Korea and China. *Asian Studies Review*, 36(2), pp. 151–170. doi:10.1080/10357823.2012.685450.

Cho, B. and Sohn, A. (2016). How Do Sexual Identity, and Coming Out Affect Stress, Depression, and Suicidal Ideation and Attempts Among Men Who Have Sex with Men in South Korea?. *Osong Public Health and Research Perspectives*, 7(5), pp. 281–288. doi:10.1016/j.phrp.2016.09.001.

Cho, J. (S. P.) (2009). The Wedding Banquet Revisited: "Contract Marriages" between Korean Gays and Lesbians. *Anthropological Quarterly*, 82(2), pp. 401–422.

Cho, J. (S. P.). (2011) Faceless Things: South Korean Gay Men, Internet, and Sexual Citizenship. PhD. University of Illinois. Available at: https://search.proquest.com/pqdtglobal/docview/1009077934/56952540CCFA42C0PQ/1?accountid=8424.

Cho, J. (S. P.) (2020). The Luxury of Love: Neoliberal Single Gay Men in Recessionary South Korea. *GLQ: A Journal of Lesbian and Gay Studies*, 26(1), pp. 151–159. doi:10.1215/10642684-7929185.

Cho, M.-A. (2011). The Other Side of Their Zeal. *Theology & Sexuality*, 17(3), pp. 297–318. doi:10.1179/tas.17.3.xx56t21243207121.

Choi, A., Calero, J., and Escardíbul, J.-O. (2012). Private Tutoring and Academic Achievement in Korea: An approach through PISA-2006. *KEDI Journal of Educational Policy*, 9(2), pp. 300–322.

Choy, B. Y. (1979). Koreans in America. Chicago: Nelson-Hall, Inc.

Chung, A. (2018). Foreign student numbers grow a record 19% in a year, University World News. [Online] University World News. Available at: https://www.universityworldnews.com/post.php?story=20181011124906535 (Accessed: December 1, 2020).

Chung, Y. B. and Katayama, M. (1998). Ethnic and Sexual Identity Development of Asian-American Lesbian and Gay Adolescents. *Professional School Counseling*, 1(3), pp. 21–25.

Chung, Y. B. and Szymanski, D. M. (2006). Racial and Sexual Identities of Asian American Gay Men. *Journal of LGBT Issues in Counseling*, 1(2), pp. 67–93. doi:10.1300/J462v01n02_05.

Clark, D. N. (1986). *Christianity in Modern Korea*. New York: University Press of America.

Cochran, S. D. et al. (2007). Mental Health and Substance Use Disorders among Latino and Asian American Lesbian, Gay, and Bisexual Adults. *Journal of Consulting and Clinical Psychology*, 75(5), pp. 785–794. doi:https://doi.org/10.1037/0022-006X.75.5.785.

Coleman, E. J. and Chou, W.-S. (2000). *Tongzhi: Politics of Same-Sex Eroticism in Chinese Societies*. New York: Routledge. doi:10.4324/9780203057056.

Cortell, A. P. and Davis, J. W. (1996). How Do International Institutions Matter? The Domestic Impact of International Rules and Norms. *International Studies Quarterly*, 40(4), pp. 451–478. doi:10.2307/2600887.

Crenshaw, K. (1989). Demarginalizing the Intersection of Race and Sex: A Black Feminist Critique of Antidiscrimination Doctrine, Feminist Theory and Antiracist Politics. *University of Chicago Legal Forum*, 1989(1), pp. 139–168.

Delgado, R. and Stefancic, J. (2017). *Critical Race Theory: An Introduction*. 3rd ed. New York: New York University Press.

Duggan, L. (2002). The New Homonormativity: The Sexual Politics of Neoliberalism. In: R. Castronovo, and D. D. Nelson, eds., *Materializing Democracy: Toward a Revitalized Cultural Politics*. Durham: Duke University Press (New Americanists), pp. 175–194.

Eble, C. (2017). College Slang and the A-Curve. *American Speech*, 92(1), pp. 92–100. doi:10.1215/00031283-4153241.

Edgar, E.-A. (2011). "Xtravaganza!": Drag Representation and Articulation in "RuPaul's Drag Race." *Studies in Popular Culture*, 34(1), pp. 133–146.

Eguchi, S. (2011). Cross-National Identity Transformation: Becoming a Gay "Asian-American" Man. *Sexuality & Culture*, 15(1), pp. 19–40. doi:10.1007/s12119-010-9080-z.

Fa'avae, D., Jones, A. and Manu'atu, L. (2016) Talanoa'i 'A e Talanoa—Talking about Talanoa: Some Dilemmas of a Novice Researcher, *AlterNative: An International Journal of Indigenous Peoples*, 12(2), pp. 138–150. Available at: https://doi.org/10.20507/AlterNative.2016.12.2.3.

Fa'avae, D. T. M., Faleolo, R., Havea, H., Enari, D., Wright, T., and Chand, A. (2022). e-talanoa as an Online Research Method: Extending Vā-relations across Spaces. *AlterNative: An International Journal of Indigenous Peoples*, 18(3), pp. 391–401. Available at: https://doi.org/10.1177/11771801221118609.

Foucault, M. et al. (1991). *The Foucault Effect: Studies in Governmentality*. Chicago: University of Chicago Press. doi:10.7208/chicago/9780226028811.001.0001.

Friedman, E. J. (2012). Constructing "The Same Rights with the Same Names": The Impact of Spanish Norm Diffusion on Marriage Equality in Argentina. *Latin American Politics and Society*, 54(4), pp. 29–59. doi:10.1111/j.1548-2456.2012.00171.x.

Fung, R. (2005). Looking for My Penis: The Eroticized Asian in Gay Video Porn. In: K. A. Ono, ed., *A Companion to Asian American Studies*. New York: John Wiley & Sons, pp. 235–253.

Giwa, D. S. (2022). *Racism and Gay Men of Color: Living and Coping with Discrimination*. Lanham, MD: Rowman & Littlefield.

Gomillion, S. C. and Giuliano, T. A. (2011). The Influence of Media Role Models on Gay, Lesbian, and Bisexual Identity. *Journal of Homosexuality*, 58(3), pp. 330–354. doi:10.1080/00918369.2011.546729.

Goodman, R. and Jinks, D. (2004). How to Influence States: Socialization and International Human Rights Law. *Duke Law Journal*, 54(3), pp. 621–723.

Gordon, J. (2005). Inadvertent Complicity: Colorblindness in Teacher Education. *Educational Studies*, 38(2), pp. 135–153. doi:10.1207/s15326993es3802_5.

Grewal, I. and Kaplan, C. (2001). Global Identities: Theorizing Transnational Studies of Sexuality. *GLQ: A Journal of Lesbian and Gay Studies*, 7(4), pp. 663–679.

Guzman, A. T. (2008). *How International Law Works: A Rational Choice Theory*. Oxford; New York: Oxford University Press.

Han, C. (2007). They Don't Want to Cruise Your Type: Gay Men of Color and the Racial Politics of Exclusion. *Social Identities*, 13(1), pp. 51–67. doi:10.1080/13504630601163379.

Han, C. (2008a). No Fats, Femmes, or Asians: The Utility of Critical Race Theory in Examining the Role of Gay Stock Stories in the Marginalization of Gay Asian Men. *Contemporary Justice Review*, 11(1), pp. 11–22. doi:10.1080/10282580701850355.

Han, C. (2008b). Sexy like a Girl and Horny like a Boy: Contemporary Gay "Western" Narratives about Gay Asian Men. *Critical Sociology*, 34(6), pp. 829–850. doi:10.1177/0896920508095101.

Han, C. and Choi, K.-H. (2018). Very Few People Say "No Whites": Gay Men of Color and the Racial Politics of Desire. *Sociological Spectrum*, 38(3), pp. 145–161. doi:10.1080/02732173.2018.1469444.

Han, W. (2018). Proud of Myself as LGBTQ: The Seoul Pride Parade, Homonationalism and Queer Developmental Citizenship. *Korea Journal*, 58(2), pp. 27–57.

Harris, A., Battle, J., and Pastrana, A. J. (2017). *An Examination of Asian and Pacific Islander LGBT Populations Across the United States: Intersections of Race and Sexuality*. New York, NY: Palgrave Macmillan (Palgrave pivot).

Henry, T. A. (ed.) (2020). *Queer Korea*. Durham: Duke University Press (Perverse modernities).

Jackson, S., Liu, J. and Woo, J. (2013). *East Asian Sexualities: Modernity, Gender and New Sexual Cultures*. London: ZED.

Jang, S. M. and Lee, H. (2014). When Pop Music Meets a Political Issue: Examining How "Born This Way" Influences Attitudes Toward

Gays and Gay Rights Policies. *Journal of Broadcasting & Electronic Media*, 58(1), pp. 114–130. doi:10.1080/08838151.2013.875023.

Keil, M. (2021). Navigating Gendered Relational Spaces in Talanoa: Centering Gender in Talanoa Research Methodology. *The Journal of New Zealand Studies* [Preprint], (NS33). Available at: https://doi.org/10.26686/jnzs.iNS33.7384.

Kim, C. S. (2011). *Voices of Foreign Brides: The Roots and Development of Multiculturalism in Korea*. Lanham, MD: Rowman & Littlefield Publishers.

Kim, E. J. (2010). *Adopted Territory: Transnational Korean Adoptees and the Politics of Belonging*. London: Duke University Press.

Kim, M. and Strauss, S. (2018). Emergent Multiplicities of Self- and Other-construction in Korean Workplace-based Television Dramas. *Journal of Pragmatics,* 137, pp. 19–36. doi:10.1016/j.pragma.2018.08.021.

Kim, Y.-G. and Hahn, S.-J. (2006). Homosexuality in Ancient and Modern Korea. *Culture, Health & Sexuality*, 8(1), pp. 59–65. doi:10.1080/13691050500159720.

König, M. (2000). Religion and the Nation-State in South Korea: A Case of Changing Interpretations of Modernity in a Global Context. *Social Compass*, 47(4), pp. 551–570. doi:10.1177/003776800047004008.

Lee, H.-K. (2018). Self-referring in Korean, with Reference to Korean First-person Markers. In: M. Huang and K. M. Jaszczolt, eds., *Expressing the Self: Cultural Diversity and Cognitive Universals*. Oxford: Oxford University Press, pp. 58–71.

Lee, I. (2011). Teaching How to Discriminate: Globalization, Prejudice, and Textbooks. *Teacher Education Quarterly*, 38(1), pp. 47–63.

Lee, I. (2016). Homoeroticism and Homosexuality in Korean Confucian Culture. *Sacred Spaces*, 8, pp. 75–94.

Leong, R. (ed.) (1996). *Asian American Sexualities: Dimensions of the Gay and Lesbian Experience*. New York: Routledge.

Li, E. P. H., Min, H. J. and Belk, R. W. (2008). Skin Lightening and Beauty in Four Asian Cultures. *NA – Advances in Consumer Research*. Edited by Lee, A. Y. and Soman, D., 35, pp. 444–449.

Lim, H. S. and Johnson, M. M. (2001). Korean Social Work Students' Attitudes Toward Homosexuals. *Journal of Social Work Education*, 37(3), pp. 545–554. doi:10.1080/10437797.2001.10779073.

Liu, P. (2007). Queer Marxism in Taiwan. *Inter-Asia Cultural Studies*, 8(4), pp. 517–539. doi:10.1080/14649370701567971.

Longres, J. F. (ed.) (1996). *Men of Color: A Context for Service to Homosexually Active Men*. New York: Haworth Press.

Lopesi, L. (2021). *Bloody Woman*. Bridget Williams Books. Available at: https://doi.org/10.7810/9781988587998.

Moon, S. (2005). *Militarized Modernity and Gendered Citizenship in South Korea*. Durham, NC: Duke University Press (Politics, history, and culture).

Narui, M. (2011). Understanding Asian/American Gay, Lesbian, and Bisexual Experiences from a Poststructural Perspective. *Journal of Homosexuality*, 58(9), pp. 1211–1234. doi:10.1080/00918369.2011.605734.

Ocampo, A. C. and Soodjinda, D. (2016). Invisible Asian Americans: The Intersection of Sexuality, Race, and Education among Gay Asian Americans. *Race Ethnicity and Education*, 19(3), pp. 480–499. doi:10.1080/13613324.2015.1095169.

Park, K. (1997). *The Korean American Dream: Immigrants and Small Business in New York City*. Ithaca, NY: Cornell University Press (Anthropology of contemporary issues).

Patton, M. J. (1991). Qualitative Research on College Students: Philosophical and Methodological Comparisons with the Quantitative Approach. *Journal of College Student Development*, 32(5), pp. 389–396.

Phua, V. C. (2007). Contesting and Maintaining Hegemonic Masculinities: Gay Asian American Men in Mate Selection. *Sex Roles*, 57(11), pp. 909–918. doi:10.1007/s11199-007-9318-x.

Puar, J. K. (2007). *Terrorist Assemblages: Homonationalism in Queer Times*. Durham, NC: Duke University Press.

Puar, J. K. (2013). Rethinking Homonationalism. *International Journal of Middle East Studies*, 45(2), pp. 336–339. doi:10.1017/S002074381300007X.

Puar, J. K. (2016). Homonationalism as Assemblage: Viral Travels, Affective Sexualities. *Revista Lusófona de Estudos Culturais*, 3(1), pp. 319–337.

Pyke, K. D. (2010). What Is Internalized Racial Oppression and Why Don't We Study It? Acknowledging Racism's Hidden Injuries. *Sociological Perspectives*, 53(4), pp. 551–572. doi:10.1525/sop.2010.53.4.551.

Pyle, J. J. (1998). Race, Equality and the Rule of Law: Critical Race Theory's Attack on the Promises of Liberalism. *BCL Rev*, 70, p. 787.

Roberts, T. and Andrews, D. J. C. (2013). A Critical Race Analysis of the Gaslighting Against African American Teachers Considerations for Recruitment and Retention. In: D. C. Andrews, and F. Tuitt, eds., *Contesting the Myth of a "Post Racial Era": The Continued Significance of Race in U.S. Education*. New York: Peter Lang (Black studies and critical thinking, Vol. 28), pp. 69–94.

Seo, D. (2001). Mapping the Vicissitudes of Homosexual Identities in South Korea. *Journal of Homosexuality*, 40(3–4), pp. 65–78. doi:10.1300/J082v40n03_04.

Seol, D.-H. (2012). The Citizenship of Foreign Workers in South Korea. *Citizenship Studies*, 16(1), pp. 119–133. doi:10.1080/13621025.2012.651408.

Slaughter, A.-M. (1995). International Law in a World of Liberal States. *European Journal of International Law*, 6(3), pp. 503–538. doi:10.1093/oxfordjournals.ejil.a035934.

Stacey, L. and Forbes, T. D. (2022). Feeling Like a Fetish: Racialized Feelings, Fetishization, and the Contours of Sexual Racism on Gay Dating Apps. *The Journal of Sex Research*, 59(3), pp. 372–384. doi:10.1080/00224499.2021.1979455.

Standen, B. C. S. (1996). Without a Template: The Biracial Korean/White Experience. In: M. P. P. Root, ed., *The Multiracial Experience: Racial Borders as the New Frontier*. Thousand Oaks, CA: Sage Publications, pp. 245–259. doi:10.4135/9781483327433.n15.

Statistics Korea. (2018). 2017 Population and Housing Census, Statistics Korea. [Online] Available at: http://kostat.go.kr/portal/eng/pressReleases/1/index.board?bmode=read&aSeq=370994 (Accessed: December 17, 2020).

Tamasese, K. et al. (2005). Ole Taeao Afua, the New Morning: A Qualitative Investigation into Samoan Perspectives on Mental Health and Culturally Appropriate Services. *Australian & New Zealand Journal of Psychiatry*, 39(4), pp. 300–309. doi:10.1080/j.1440-1614.2005.01572.x.

Teunis, N. (2007). Sexual Objectification and the Construction of Whiteness in the Gay Male Community. *Culture, Health & Sexuality*, 9(3), pp. 263–275. doi:10.1080/13691050601035597.

Thomsen, P. S. (2019). Coming-Out in the Intersections: Examining Relationality in How Korean Gay Men in Seattle Navigate Church, Culture and Family through a Pacific Lens, *Journal of Homosexuality*, pp. 1–22. Available at: https://doi.org/10.1080/00918369.2019.1695423.

Thomsen, P. S. (2020). Transnational Interest Convergence and Global Korea at the Edge of Race and Queer Experiences: A Talanoa with Gay Men in Seoul, Du Bois Review: Social Science Research on Race, pp. 1–18. Available at: https://doi.org/10.1017/S1742058X20000247.

Thomsen, P. S. (2022). Research "Side-Spaces" and the Criticality of Auckland, New Zealand, as a Site for Developing a Queer Pacific Scholarly Agenda. *New Zealand Sociology*, 37(1), pp. 120–142.

Thomsen, P. S., Lopesi, L., and Lee, K. (2022). Contemporary Moana Mobilities: Settler-Colonial Citizenship, Upward Mobility, and Transnational Pacific Identities. *The Contemporary Pacific*, 34(2), pp. 326–351.

Troiden, R. R. (1989). The Formation of Homosexual Identities. *Journal of Homosexuality*, 17(1–2), pp. 43–74. doi:10.1300/J082v17n01_02.

Tsunokai, G. T., McGrath, A. R. and Kavanagh, J. K. (2014). Online Dating Preferences of Asian Americans. *Journal of Social and Personal Relationships*, 31(6), pp. 796–814. doi:10.1177/0265407513505925.

Um, N.-H., Kim, J. M. and Kim, S. (2016). Korea Out of the Closet: Effects of Gay-themed Ads on Young Korean Consumers. *Asian Journal of Communication*, 26(3), pp. 240–261. doi:10.1080/01292986.2016.1144774.

Vaioleti, T. M. (2006). Talanoa Research Methodology: A Developing Position on Pacific Research. *Waikato Journal of Education*, 12(1), pp. 21–34. doi:10.15663/wje.v12i1.296.

Wagner, B. K. and Van Volkenburg, M. (2012). HIV/AIDS Tests as a Proxy for Racial Discrimination – A Preliminary Investigation of South Korea's Policy of Mandatory In-Country HIV/AIDS Tests for Its Foreign English Teachers. *Journal of Korean Law*, 11(2), pp. 179–246.

Wang, F. T. Y., Bih, H.-D., and Brennan, D. J. (2009). Have They Really Come Out: Gay Men and Their Parents in Taiwan. *Culture, Health & Sexuality*, 11(3), pp. 285–296. doi:10.1080/13691050802572711.

Wendt, A. (1996). *Tatauing the Post-Colonial Body*. [Online] NZEPC. Available at: http://www.nzepc.auckland.ac.nz/authors/wendt/tatauing.asp (Accessed: December 17, 2020).

Wolf, M. (1972). *Women and the Family in Rural Taiwan*. Stanford, CA: Stanford University Press.

Wozolek, B. (2018). Gaslighting Queerness: Schooling as a Place of Violent Assemblages. *Journal of LGBT Youth*, 15(4), pp. 319–338. doi:10.1080/19361653.2018.1484839.

Yang, H. (ed.) (2013). *Law and Society in Korea*. Cheltenham, UK; Northampton, MA, USA: Edward Elgar (Elgar Korean law series).

Yeoh, B. S. A., Willis, K. D. and Fakhri, S. M. A. K. (2003). Introduction: Transnationalism and Its Edges. *Ethnic and Racial Studies*, 26(2), pp. 207–217. doi:10.1080/0141987032000054394.

Young, S. L. (2009). Half and Half: An (Auto)ethnography of Hybrid Identities in a Korean American Mother-Daughter Relationship. *Journal of International and Intercultural Communication*, 2(2), pp. 139–167. doi:10.1080/17513050902759512.

Recommended further reading

Cho, J. (Song P. (2020). The Luxury of Love: Neoliberal Single Gay Men in Recessionary South Korea, *GLQ: A Journal of Lesbian and Gay Studies*, 26(1), pp. 151–159. Available at: https://doi.org/10.1215/10642684-7929185.

Giwa, D.S. (2022) *Racism and Gay Men of Color: Living and Coping with Discrimination*. Rowman & Littlefield.

Han, E.-J., Han, M.W., and Lee, J. (2021) *Korean diaspora across the world: homeland in history, memory, imagination, media, and reality*.

Han, C. and Choi, K.-H. (2018) Very Few People Say "No Whites": Gay Men of Color and the Racial Politics of Desire, *Sociological Spectrum*, 38(3), pp. 145–161. Available at: https://doi.org/10.1080/02732173.2018.1469444.

Henry, T.A. (ed.) (2020) *Queer Korea*. Durham: Duke University Press (Perverse modernities).

Index

Confucian
  familism 5, 7–9, 36–38, 42, 68, 108, 179
Critical race theory 13, 176, 178, 181
  interest convergence 30

Discourse 6, 15, 67, 79, 110, 154, 168

Familism 7–9, 41, 44, 47, 67, 103–105, 112, 163
  affectionate familism 8
  individual familism 8–9
  Instrumental 8

Gay v–1, 3–4, 7, 9–11, 14–16, 18, 26–31, 34, 40–42, 47, 51–53, 58–61, 63, 66, 68–71, 75–85, 87–91, 94, 96, 99–100, 102–109, 111–112, 115–124, 126–127, 130, 136–147, 149–150, 152, 154–155, 157–164, 166–170
  identity 5, 9, 14, 16–20, 28, 36–37, 39, 41, 43, 45, 47, 51, 56, 61–62, 66–68, 70, 75–77, 85, 89, 92, 95, 102, 105, 107–108, 112, 117,
    120, 127, 129, 143–144, 154, 160–161, 163, 166
  masculinity 57, 82
  stereotype 83
  subjectivity 5, 9, 41, 60–61, 70, 82–83, 91, 100, 142, 162–163

Heteronormativity 141, 159
  heterosexism 53, 82, 108, 141
Homonationalism 14–15, 95–96, 119, 164
Homonormativity 15, 17, 119

Intersectionality 13, 117

Marginalization 5, 70, 122, 149, 158
Masculinity
  demasculinization 117
Masculinity
  toxic 57

Racism v, 11–13, 30–31, 95, 115–116, 118–120, 122–125, 128, 130, 137–138, 140, 147, 149, 153, 155, 158, 164–165

Racism

  colorblind 124

  Interpersonal 14, 19, 31

  Structural 14, 30–31, 67, 136,
  138, 155, 167

Talanoa v, 20–21, 26–27, 30,
  33–34, 36–37, 41, 44, 46, 49,
  55, 58, 65, 67–68, 77, 80–81,
  84, 86, 88, 93, 100, 103, 107,
  124–125, 136, 139–140, 142,
  168

  story telling 118

Transnational 4, 11, 28, 31, 60–61,
  63, 66–67, 71, 112, 125, 128,
  130, 155, 159–162, 164,
  167–168, 178

  connection 25, 30, 34, 38–39,
  44, 50, 56, 79, 102, 112, 123,
  137

  mobility 4, 63, 125, 128, 159